SHEPHERD'S NOTES

SHEPHERD'S NOTES

When you need a guide through the Scriptures

I & II
Thessalonians

BROADMAN
&HOLMAN
PUBLISHERS

Nashville, Tennessee

1–55819–714–1
Dewey Decimal Classification: 227.8
Subject Heading: BIBLE. N.T. THESSALONIANS
Library of Congress Card Catalog Number: 97-32426

Library of Congress Cataloging-in-Publication Data
1,2 Thessalonians.
  p. cm. — (Shepherd's notes)
  Includes bibliographical references.
  ISBN 0–8054–9000–0
  1. Bible. N.T. Thessalonians—Study and teaching. I. Series.
BS2725.5.A19 1997
227'.81'007—dc21
                     97-32426
                      CIP

1 2 3 4 5 6 03 02 01 00 99 98

CONTENTS

FOREWORD

Dear Reader:

Shepherd's Notes are designed to give you a quick, step-by-step overview of every book of the Bible. They are not meant to be substitutes for the biblical text; rather, they are study guides intended to help you explore the wisdom of Scripture in personal or group study and to apply that wisdom successfully in your own life.

Shepherd's Notes guide you through the main themes of each book of the Bible and illuminate fascinating details through appropriate commentary and reference notes. Historical and cultural background information brings the Bible into sharper focus.

Six different icons, used throughout the series, call your attention to historical-cultural information, Old Testament and New Testament references, word pictures, unit summaries, and personal application for everyday life.

Whether you are a novice or a veteran at Bible study, I believe you will find *Shepherd's Notes* a resource that will take you to a new level in your mining and applying the riches of Scripture.

In Him,

David R. Shepherd
Editor-in-Chief

HOW TO USE THIS BOOK

DESIGNED FOR THE BUSY USER

Shepherd's Notes for 1, 2 Thessalonians is designed to provide an easy-to-use tool for getting a quick handle on the important features of these Bible books, and for gaining an understanding of the message of 1, 2 Thessalonians. Information available in more difficult-to-use reference works has been incorporated into the *Shepherd's Notes* format. This brings you the benefits of many more advanced and expensive works packed into one small volume.

Shepherd's Notes are for laymen, pastors, teachers, small-group leaders and participants, as well as the classroom student. Enrich your personal study or quiet time. Shorten your class or small-group preparation time as you gain valuable insights into the truths of God's Word that you can pass along to your students or group members.

DESIGNED FOR QUICK ACCESS

Bible students with time constraints will especially appreciate the timesaving features built in the *Shepherd's Notes*. All features are intended to aid a quick and concise encounter with the heart of the message.

Concise Commentary. First and 2 Thessalonians are replete with both doctrinal and ethical instruction to believers. Short sections provide quick "snapshots" of sections, highlighting important points and other information.

Outlined Text. A comprehensive outline covers the entire text of 1, 2 Thessalonians. This is a valuable feature for following the narrative's flow, allowing for a quick, easy way to locate a particular passage.

Shepherd's Notes. These summary statements appear at the close of every key section of the narrative. While functioning in part as a quick summary, they also deliver the essence of the message presented in the sections which they cover.

Icons. Various icons in the margin highlight recurring themes in 1, 2 Thessalonians and aid in selective searching or tracing of those themes.

Sidebars and Charts. These specially selected features provide additional background information to your study or preparation. These include definitions as well as cultural, historical, and biblical insights.

Maps. These are placed at appropriate places in the book to aid your understanding and study of a text or passage.

Questions to Guide Your Study. These thought-provoking questions and discussion starters are designed to encourage interaction with the truth and principles of God's Word.

In addition to the above features, study aids have been included at the back of the book for those readers who require or desire more information and resources for working through 1, 2 Thessalonians. These include:

- chapter outlines for studying 1, 2 Thessalonians
- a list of reference sources used for this volume, which offer many works that allow the reader to extend the scope of his or her study of 1, 2 Thessalonians.

DESIGNED TO WORK FOR YOU
Personal Study. Using *Shepherd's Notes* with a passage of Scripture can enlighten your study and take it to a new level. At your fingertips is information that would require searching several volumes to find. In addition, many points of application occur throughout the volume, contributing to personal growth.

Teaching. Outlines frame the text of 1 and 2 Thessalonians providing a logical presentation of the message. Capsule thoughts designated as "Shepherd's Notes" provide summary statements for presenting the essence of key points and events. Personal application icons point out personal application of Paul's message in 1, 2 Thessalonians, and Historical context icons indicate where background information is supplied.

Group Study. Shepherd's Notes can be an excellent companion volume to use for gaining a quick but accurate understanding of the message of a Bible book. Each group member can benefit by having his or her own copy. The *Note's* format accommodates the study of or the tracing of the themes throughout 1, 2 Thessalonians. Leaders may use its flexible features to prepare for group sessions, or use them during group sessions. Questions to guide your study can spark discussion of the key points and truths of 1, 2 Thessalonians.

LIST OF MARGIN ICONS USED IN 1, 2 THESSALONIANS

 Shepherd's Notes. Placed at the end of each section, a capsule statement provides the reader with the essence of the message of that section.

 Old Testament Reference. Used when the writer refers to Old Testament Scripture passages that are related or have a bearing on the passage's understanding or interpretation.

 New Testament Reference. Used when the writer refers to New Testament passages that are related to or have a bearing on the passage's understanding or interpretation.

 Historical Background. To indicate historical, cultural, geographical, or biographical information that sheds light on the understanding or interpretation of a passage.

 Personal Application. Used when the text provides a personal or universal application of truth.

 Word Picture. Indicates that the meaning of a specific word or phrase is illustrated so as to shed light on it.

FIRST THESSALONIANS

Galatians probably was the first letter Paul wrote, and 1 Thessalonians was the second. Paul traveled to Thessalonica on his second missionary journey around A.D. 51. Luke reported this brief visit, Paul's preaching ministry there with Silas, and the subsequent persecution that drove him and his companions out of the city (Acts 17:1–9). Many people believed in Jesus Christ before they were compelled to leave.

From Thessalonica, Paul went to Berea and Athens, and then to Corinth. Timothy and Silas, who had been with Paul at Thessalonica, rejoined him in Corinth. Paul wrote 1 Thessalonians in response to Timothy's report shortly after his arrival.

1 Thessalonians in a "Nutshell"

Purpose	To encourage new converts during persecution; to instruct them in Christian living and to assure them concerning the Second Coming.
Major Doctrine	Last Things
Key Passage	1 Thess. 4:13–18
Other Key Doctrines	Evangelism, prayer, and God
Influence of the Letter	Every chapter of 1 Thessalonians ends with a reference to the Second Coming of Christ

Thessalonica, the capital of Macedonia, was larger than Philippi. It was a free city, having no Roman garrison within its walls. Like Corinth, it was a cosmopolitan city.

"His [Paul's] signature at the close was the proof of genuineness (2 Thess. 3:17) against all spurious claimants (2 Thess. 2:2). Unfortunately the brittle papyrus on which he wrote easily perished outside of the sand heaps and tombs of Egypt or the lava covered ruins of Herculaneum. What a treasure that autograph would be!"

A.T. Robertson, *Word Pictures in the New Testament,* vol. 4, 5–6.

Author

Both 1 and 2 Thessalonians claim Paul as author. The vocabulary, style, and theology are Paul's. No decisive objections to Paul's authorship have swayed the convictions of centuries of Christian opinion.

Purpose for Writing

Paul received the report that the Thessalonians were strong in faith and were making favorable progress. After receiving this information about the church, Paul wrote 1 Thessalonians to accomplish several purposes:

He wanted to encourage believers as they stood firm against intense persecution (1 Thess. 2:14; 3:1–4).

He responded to criticism against his motives in Christian service by explaining how he had conducted his ministry in Thessalonica (1 Thess. 2:1–12).

The presence of low moral standards in Thessalonica led Paul to explain Christian standards for sexual purity (1 Thess. 4:1–8).

The death of some members in the congregation sparked questions about how deceased members would participate in the coming return of Christ, and Paul answered their questions (1 Thess. 4:13–18).

The church needed instruction about the appropriate use of spiritual gifts (1 Thess. 5:19–22).

Place and Date of Writing

First Thessalonians was probably written while Paul was in Corinth.

Some have suggested that 2 Thessalonians was written before 1 Thessalonians. Neither letter claims to come before the other, and it is also possible that this suggestion is correct.

Audience
Paul's readership was the congregation in the church at Thessalonica. Since Paul's ministry there, the church had grown, according to the report Timothy brought to Paul. But the church was experiencing persecution. The believers were new converts, and they were in need of encouragement to remain faithful under these pressures.

Theological Significance of 1 Thessalonians
The letter is more practical than theological. It is God-centered throughout. God chose the Thessalonians unto salvation (1 Thess. 1:4). His will is the guide for all believers (4:3). He calls His people to holy living (4:7) and enables them to live obediently. He raised Jesus from the dead (4:14) and will raise believers to be with Him at the Lord's return (4:13–5:11).

This letter was written specifically to reassure those who were concerned about believers who had already died.

Basic Outline of 1 Thessalonians
I. Salutation (1:1)
II. Personal Relations (1:2–3:13)
III. Church Problems (4:1–5:11)
IV. Concluding Exhortations (5:12–28)

The letter can be dated with the help of the Delphi Inscription, which provides information about the service of the proconsul Gallio. Gallio probably assumed office in the summer of A.D. 51 and served through the summer of A.D. 52. Paul was brought before Gallio shortly after the governor's arrival in Corinth, near the end of Paul's eighteen-month stay in the city (Acts 18:9–18). Paul's Corinthian ministry probably began in A.D. 50, and Paul wrote 1 Thessalonians either in this year or the following year.

Words of comfort and hope from Paul about the resurrection of believers provide equally good news for the church at all times in all places. This good news serves as a basis for practical and godly living.

SECOND THESSALONIANS

Paul's second letter to the Thessalonians was apparently evoked by alarm on the part of believers who had been informed that the day of the Lord had arrived. The agitator who had confused the Thessalonians apparently appealed for authority either to the utterances of inspired prophets within the church, or to some phrases from Paul's writings, or possibly to a forged letter (2 Thess. 2:1–2). Some who anticipated the Lord's imminent return had stopped working and were depending on others to supply them with life's necessities (3:11).

Because of inexperience, the church members were uncertain of their position. They needed reassurance to cope with the opposition of pagan culture and with doubts raised by their misunderstandings (2:15), and discipline was needed to keep the lazy members from disrupting community life (3:13–15).

2 Thessalonians in a "Nutshell"

Purpose	To encourage new converts in persecution and to correct their misunderstanding about the Lord's return.
Major Doctrine	Last Things
Key Passage	1 Thess. 1:3–12
Other Key Doctrines	Prayer, the church, evil, and suffering
Influence of the Letter	With only three chapters, the letter is one of Paul's shortest. But because of 2:3–10, it is one the most extensively studied.

Author

In 2 Thessalonians 1:1 we read, "Paul, Silas, and Timothy." Some scholars have questioned

Paul's authorship of 2 Thessalonians because of variations with the doctrine of Christ's return as presented in 1 Thessalonians. However, as with Paul's authorship of 1 Thessalonians, no decisive objections have changed centuries of Christian opinion about Pual's authorship.

Purpose for Writing

Paul's purpose in writing 2 Thessalonians paralleled his first letter to these believers. Several reasons for this letter are prominent:

- He wrote to encourage the persecuted church (1:4–10).

- He attempted to correct their misunderstanding about the Lord's return.

- He exhorted the church to be steadfast in all things (2:13–3:15).

- Paul's emphasis was on the return of Christ when the church would be gathered to Him (2:1), and the wicked would be judged (1:6–9; 2:8).

- Paul also instructed the church concerning the man of lawlessness (2:1–12).

Date of Writing

Assuming that Paul was the author along with the traditional sequence of the two letters, 2 Thessalonians would be dated several months after the writing of 1 Thessalonians, This would place the date of writing toward the end of Paul's Corinthian ministry—late A.D. 50 or early A.D. 51.

Audience

The audience was the same as 1 Thessalonians. (See "Audience" for 1 Thess. above.)

We must be prepared, for He will come as suddenly as a thief in the night. Those who have died and those who are still alive will be united with Christ at His return. These words provide hope and encouragement for the church at all times.

Theological Significance of 2 Thessalonians

The emphasis of this epistle on the Second Coming of Christ reminds us to be ready for Christ's coming at any time.

Likewise, we must be alert to the evil schemes of the man of lawlessness. The church gains strength from the instruction about the wicked activity of Satan with his power and pretended signs and wonders. Believers are empowered with the truth that the man of lawlessness will be finally destroyed by the Lord Jesus at His coming (2 Thess. 2:12). In the meantime, the church must remain faithful and steadfast to the goodwill and providential purposes of God.

Basic Outline of 2 Thessalonians

   I. Salutation (1:1–2)
   II. Encouragement for the Church (1:3–12)
   III. Instructions to Correct Misunderstandings
       (2:1–12)
   IV. Injunctions to Steadfastness (2:13–3:18)

MAJOR THEMES IN THE THESSALONIAN LETTERS

Persecution and peace. Both Thessalonian letters deal with the problem of persecution of the church. Both begin and conclude with Paul's concern of peace for the Thessalonian believers.

The end-times and endurance. Several sections of both letters address various aspects of the end-times. In 1 Thessalonians, Paul comforted grieving believers in the church, whereas in 2 Thessalonians he assured the persecuted church that their persecutors would suffer punishment.

Election and faith. The word for *church* refers to people who are "called out." These people are chosen by God (1 Thess. 1:4). Along with the reality of God's sovereignty Paul recognized the reality of the human response—faith.

QUESTIONS TO GUIDE YOUR STUDY

1. What prompted Paul to write 1 Thessalonians? Second Thessalonians?
2. What was Paul's goal in writing 1 Thessalonians? Second Thessalonians?
3. What were the Thessalonian believers like? What had been their history with Paul?
4. What major doctrines does Paul address in the Thessalonian letters?

City of Thessalonica

Cassander, a general of Alexander the Great, founded the city of Thessalonica in 315 B.C., naming it after his wife. Located on the Thermaic Gulf (Gulf of Salonika) with an excellent harbor—and at the termination of a major trade route from the Danube—it became, one of the most important commercial centers in Greece. In the Roman period, it retained its Greek cultural orientation and functioned as the capital of Macedonia after 146 B.C.

When Paul visited the city, it was larger than Philippi, which reflected a predominantly Roman culture. Thessalonica was a free city, having no Roman garrison within its walls and maintaining the privilege of minting its own coins. Like Corinth, it had a cosmopolitan population due to the commercial prowess of the city.

The Life and Ministry of Paul

MAJOR EVENTS	BIBLICAL RECORDS		POSSIBLE DATES
	Acts	Galatians	
Birth			A.D. 1
Conversion	9:1–25	1:11–17	33
First Jerusalem Visit	9:26–30	1:18–20	36
Famine	11:25–30	2:1–10?	46
First Missionary Journey	13:1 to 14:28		47–48
Apostolic council in Jerusalem	15:1–29	2:1–10?	49
Second missionary journey	15:36 to 18:21		
Letter to the Galatians			53–55
Third missionary journey	18:23 to 21:6		53–57
Letters to the Corinthians			55
Arrest and prison in Jerusalem and Caesarea	21:8 to 26:32		57
Prison in Rome	27:1 to 28:30		60–62
Letter to the Ephesians			60–62
Death			67

THE LIFE AND MINISTRY OF PAUL

The first several verses of this letter introduced the topics with which Paul's letter would deal (especially the first three chapters) and establish rapport with the readers. Paul gave thanks for the Thessalonians and affirmed the church's success. Thanksgiving and affirmation together praised past actions of the Thessalonians with the intent of encouraging the continuing growth of their Christian behavior and character.

THE SALUTATION (1:1)

Authors and Addresses (v. 1a)

The three men involved in the writing of the letter were Paul, Silas, and Timothy. Timothy joined Paul and Silas on the missionary journey that took them to Thessalonica.

Greeting (v. 1b)

Paul's greeting was simply "grace and peace to you." "Grace" is the love of God that flows toward us regardless of who we are or what we have done. It is the reason for our salvation and our relationship to God. "Peace" describes this new relationship that exists between a believer and God and among believers themselves. It is the total well-being that flows from the new life of grace. The combined effect of these two words transforms a routine "hello" into a theologically meaningful salutation.

THE THANKSGIVING (1:2–7)

Paul's expression of thanksgiving in this passage operated on several levels:

Paul began his letter with the name of the writer, the name of the recipient, a greeting, and a prayer of gratitude and intercession. This was the way letters generally began in the Hellenistic world of the first century.

(See "The Hellenistic Letter" sidebar in this book's treatment of 2 Thess. 1.)

Paul—The renowned apostle and leading personality among the three writers.

Silas—A trusted leader of the church in Jerusalem, and later Paul's companion on his second missionary journey.

Timothy—A prominent person both in Acts and in Paul's Letters. He was a resident of Lystra and a member of the church there.

1. It expressed a genuine appreciation for the faithfulness of the Thessalonian Christians.

2. The thanksgiving was a way of establishing rapport with the readers.

3. The thanksgiving praised several points of the Thessalonians' Christian character which Paul later encouraged and elaborated upon in the body of his letter.

Paul's Prayer of Gratitude (vv. 2–3)

What caused Paul to be so thankful to God? It was the "faith," "love," and "hope" of the Thessalonian church. These words describe the total response of the believer to what God has done in the past, is doing now, and will do in the future.

Faith is not assent to a code of rules or a body of dogma. It is the position of complete trust in God. The life of faith is also the life of love. One cannot be a believer without loving God and the children of God. Hope describes the eager expectation and confident waiting by the believer for the future that God has promised to His children.

"We are justified by faith, but faith produces works (Romans 6–8) as [John] the Baptist taught and as Jesus taught and as James does in James 2."

A.T. Robertson, *Word Pictures in the New Testament*, vol. 4, 8

Although Paul cited faith, love, and hope as prime Christian virtues (see 1 Thess. 5:8; 1 Cor. 13:13; Col. 1:5), they were not the focal point of verses 2–3. These virtues serve to identify that which motivates and produces Christian actions. The actions themselves are what Paul emphasized.

The "work of faith" that Paul praised here is the Christian life, specifically the deeds that result from the indwelling Spirit (Gal. 5:16–26; see also Eph. 2:10).

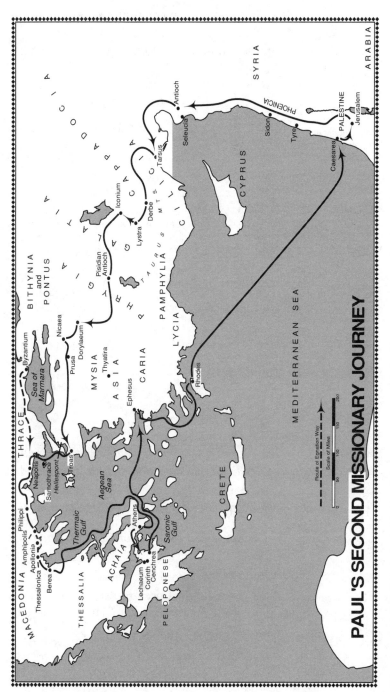

PAUL'S SECOND MISSIONARY JOURNEY

Taken from John B. Polhill, *Acts*, vol. 26, New American Commentary (Nashville, Tenn.: Broadman & Holman Publishers, 1992), p. 59

These are not prerequisites of salvation but rather the results of salvation in the lives of those who are transformed by Christ (1 Cor. 6:1–4; 12:1–2).

"Work of faith"

Edgar Goodspeed translates this phrase as "*your energetic faith.*"

Christianity in Action at Thessalonica

VIRTUE	VIRTUE IN ACTION	EXPLANATION
Faith	"work produced by faith"	Action inspired by action or carried out by faith
Love	"labor prompted by love"	Strenuous work carried out in love
Hope	"endurance inspired by hope"	Patience involved in the practice of hope

■ *After a brief greeting, Paul expressed grati-*
■ *tude for the Thessalonians' faith, love, and*
■ *hope. It was these three virtues that moti-*
■ *vated and produced their Christian actions.*

The Success of the Mission in Thessalonica (vv. 4–7)

Paul was convinced that his labors and that of his colleagues had been in keeping with God's initiative in reaching out to Thessalonian citizens—that they were chosen.

Paul had not just spoken words. God had affirmed his preaching with demonstrations of "power, with the Holy Spirit, and with deep conviction."

Power. The word Paul used here for "power" was also one of the words used by the gospel writers for Jesus' miracles. Paul's point here was that it was God's power, not his, that had been demonstrated among the Thessalonians.

Holy Spirit. The inclusion of the Holy Spirit broadened Paul's statement to more than the miraculous. The Spirit's power to call, convict, enlighten, transform, assure, and comfort is far more effective than words alone can express. In a sense, the work of the Spirit is the guarantor of truth.

Deep conviction. This may refer either to the conviction demonstrated by the missionaries or the assurance that developed in the hearers of the gospel.

- *Paul described the exemplary response of the*
- *Thessalonians to the gospel. In spite of severe*
- *suffering, the Thessalonians had a joy that*
- *could be supplied only by the Spirit. They*
- *had become imitators of Paul and the Lord,*
- *thus providing a model for all believers in*
- *Macedonia and Achaia.*

THE NEWS SPREADS (1:8–10)

The news about the response of the Thessalonian believers to the gospel spread rapidly. Indeed, this news preceded the arrival of the missionaries elsewhere. Instead of the missionaries themselves having to tell about what God had done in Thessalonica, they heard it from other people. "Everywhere" of course, is only

"Election (Gk. *ekloge*) took place "before the creation of the world" (Eph. 1:4), but its effects are seen in the life of the elect. . . . Election is a way of saying that God takes the initiative in salvation. It underscores the fact that salvation is entirely of God's grace."

David Ewart in *Evangelical Commentary on the Bible,* ed. Walter Elwell (Grand Rapids: Baker, 1989), 1070.

"Election" or "Choice"

The Greek word *eloge,* translated as "election" or "choice" occurs only seven times in the New Testament and always denotes God's choice of human beings.

A.T. Robertson, *Word Pictures in the New Testament,* vol. 4, 10.

hyperbole. Paul means "everywhere they had traveled." Even more specifically, he was probably referring to Christian places of assembly (Acts 4:31; 1 Cor. 2:1; 2 Cor. 2:14), where news of churches, persecution, and perseverance would be shared by traveling Christian merchants and missionaries.

The Thessalonians became both models (v. 7) and messengers (v. 8) of the gospel. Through their words and lives, they helped spread "the Lord's message" throughout their province, impacting the entire region of Macedonia and Achaia (see "Paul's Second Missionary Journey" in the Introduction).

Paul revealed the extent of their response to the gospel:

1. *How they received the missionaries* (v. 9). They had received the missionaries into the Thessalonian community. The difficulty and persecution associated with Paul's work in the city made the reception given by those who became believers all the more remarkable.

2. *How they turned from idols to serve God* (v. 9). Conversion is pictured here as a willful act of turning from one path and moving in another direction. The Thessalonians had turned "to God" and "from idols." This would indicate that they were pagans and not Jews.

3. *How they persistently expected the return of the Lord* (v. 10). This was the result of their genuine conversion—perseverance to the end. They awaited Jesus, who would rescue them from "the coming wrath." Believers live in anticipation of a coronation (2 Tim. 4:8) rather than a condemnation.

Because of the way the Thessalonians had received the gospel in the midst of affliction, they became a "model" for believers in Macedonia and Achaia. We do not become Christians or act like Christians by following the example of anyone. We can only be Christians by means of the presence and power of God through our personal faith. The example of the Thessalonians bore witness to the divinely given realities of a life of faith. This same course of conduct was possible to others who, inspired by the Thessalonians, also trusted God.

- *News of the response of the Thessalonian*
- *believers to the gospel had spread rapidly.*
- *They welcomed the missionaries Paul sent;*
- *they turned from idols to serve God; and they*
- *eagerly anticipated Jesus' return.*

QUESTIONS TO GUIDE YOUR STUDY

1. What is the meaning of Paul's greeting of "grace and peace"? ·
2. Why was Paul thankful for the Thessalonian Christians?
3. How were the Thessalonians a model for other believers? In what ways are they a model for believers today?
4. How had the Thessalonians responded to the gospel?

In Acts 16:12–40, we read about the planting of the church at Philippi—a church that would be a joy to Paul over the years. In this same city, on this same trip, Paul and his colleagues experienced great suffering and humiliation. Assaulted by a mob, beaten, and imprisoned, they had suffered physical pain and emotional trauma.

"Strong opposition"

The word translated "opposition" (Greek word, *agoni*) was used of the "struggle" of an athlete engaged in training or in a contest, and it was also used frequently as a metaphor for moral struggles. It speaks of the strenuous effort required to overcome an opponent. Paul did not identify the opponent in this passage. No doubt, the Thessalonians did not have to be reminded of the struggles they had encountered in the early days of their congregation.

In this section Paul presented a summary of the motivations and actions of him and his companions during their ministry in Thessalonica. He placed several statements of thanksgiving in the narrative material of chapters 2–3.

Chapter 2 was new material, but it was closely related to chapter 1 as the following chart shows.

Ties Between Chapter 1 and 2

PASSAGE IN CHAPTER 2	TREATMENT	CHAPTER 1 PASSAGE
2:1–6	expands	1:4–10
2:7–12	restates	1:5, 9
2:13–16	echoes	1:6–8, 10

THE DIFFICULTIES CONFRONTED (2:1–2)

In the preceding verses Paul wrote about the glowing reports that had gone out from Thessalonica. In chapter 2 he turned to more specific comments about the ministry of the missionaries in that city.

The missionaries' experience in Philippi prior to their arrival in Thessalonica was one of great blessing and great difficulty.

The result of their persecution was the opposite of what we might have expected. In spite of strong "opposition" in Thessalonica, the missionaries had openly and courageously proclaimed the gospel.

■ *In spite of their previous persecution in Phil-*
■ *ippi, Paul and his missionary companions*
■ *faithfully proclaimed the message which*
■ *God had entrusted to them. The success of*
■ *their mission, in spite of sustained opposi-*
■ *tion, was due largely to their courage*
■ *inspired by God.*

THE PURITY OF PAUL'S MOTIVES (2:3–5)

For some reason Paul was anxious to defend the purity of the missionaries' motives during their stay in Thessalonica. People in the Mediterranean world were accustomed to traveling philosophers, teachers, and religionists who sometimes exploited gullible people for their own gain. Perhaps the character of Paul and his companions had also been degraded by their Jewish enemies in Thessalonica.

Paul and his companions had faithfully proclaimed the message which God had entrusted to them. Faithfulness in adverse conditions is one proof of pure motives.

These witnesses, however, were responsible not only for witnessing to Paul's behavior but also for imitating it. Whether Paul was fending off an attack against the gospel, his narrative was intended to encourage the church to live as he had taught them to live.

In this passage, Paul denied two specific impure motives behind the actions of many people: greed and flattery. Paul emphasized that the readers themselves must testify to the character of him and his missionary companions. "You know" is an emphatic phrase in the text (original Greek text). The missionaries spoke not

"Approved by God"

This phrase translates one word in the original Greek text. It refers to the approval of something as the result of careful examination. The verb tense refers to a past event of testing or examination, resulting in a current state of approval. The term *approval* does imply some standard of judgment.

from any wrong motives but because God had approved them to be entrusted with the gospel.

■ *The approval of God was more significant*
■ *for Paul and his team than the success of the*
■ *mission. Paul had sufficient reason to endure*
■ *suffering and the questions surrounding his*
■ *character. He denied flattery as his means of*
■ *mission. Neither were greed and human*
■ *praise his motivations.*

GENTLE AS A NURSING MOTHER (2:6–8)

The Thessalonians might have expected Paul and his team to exert their rights and authority as "apostles of Christ." After all, they were commissioned and sent out by the Lord Himself. Instead of "making their weight felt" (NEB), the evangelists were "gentle . . . like a mother caring for her little children."

Paul was painting a word picture of his relationship to the Thessalonians. It was characterized not by his authoritarian assertion of his desires but of gentle kindness demonstrated by a mother who nurses a small baby.

The great love that the missionaries grew to feel for their Thessalonian converts could be seen in their ministry in their city. Not only were they glad to share the gospel, but they were willing to share their "lives" as well.

The Missionaries' Assertions of Love*

Assertion	Proof
1."We never used flattery, nor did we put on a mask to cover up greed" (v. 5).	1. "You know" 2. "God is our witness"
2. "We were not looking for praise from men, not from you or anyone else" (v. 6).	"As apostles of Christ we could have been a burden to you."
3. "But we were gentle among you, like a mother caring for her little children"(v. 7b).	"We loved you so much"
4. "We were delighted to share with you not only the gospel of God but our lives as well" (v. 8b).	"Because you had become so dear to us"

*(Chart taken from D. Michael Martin, 1, 2 Thessalonians (The New American Commentary), p. 80.)

■ *Rather than exhibiting flattery, greed, and*
■ *exploitation, Paul and his coworkers demon-*
■ *strated pure motives and a parental gentle-*
■ *ness born of love.*

THE UNSELFISHNESS OF THEIR LABOR (2:9–12)

In verse 9 Paul elaborated on the way in which the missionaries had shared their lives with the Thessalonians. They had engaged in strenuous, difficult manual labor to support themselves so that they would not have to be a financial burden to any of the converts.

Verses 9–10 paint a picture of a self-reliant, considerate, and righteous missionary. Paul's use of another family analogy—a father—added

The Positive Actions of the Missionaries

ACTION	VERSE
Gentleness	v. 7
Love and a desire to share the good things of the gospel	v. 8
Hard work and financial independence	v. 9
Holiness, righteousness, and blamelessness	v. 10

warmth and a personal touch to the depiction of his relationship with the Thessalonian church.

A good father encourages and provides guidance, and he is concerned about the moral development of his children. Moral problems were especially acute among believers newly won from pagan religions. Such was the case in Thessalonica. They did not have the benefit of moral training as did the Jews. Ignorance of Christian ethics, the pull of the old life, and the pressures of heathen society combined to hinder some believers from leading lives worthy of the gospel.

That is why so much of Paul's letter was dedicated to basic moral exhortation. Paul believed that one of his basic responsibilities was to support new converts in their Christian life through exhortation and encouragement. High moral standards were in keeping with the high calling believers had received from God.

■ *Paul's behavior resembled a father offering*
■ *help to his struggling children. To the hesi-*
■ *tant he offered exhortation; to the weary he*

- *offered encouragement; to the weak he*
- *offered strength and direction. His motiva-*
- *tion was to help each convert see what it*
- *meant to "live lives worthy of God, who calls*
- *you into his kingdom."*

THE ACCEPTANCE OF THE MESSAGE (2:13–16)

The missionaries had been true, honorable, and loving in their ministry. Likewise, the Thessalonian believers had been responsive to the proclamation of the gospel. So many of their neighbors had dismissed the missionaries' message as "the word of men."

But when the message was preached to the Thessalonian believers, their subsequent experience confirmed that the message was indeed "the word of God," for it continued to be "at work" in them.

Previously Paul had mentioned that his readers had experienced affliction when they received the word. He now revealed that the affliction was persecution from their own people. Paul saw his own persecution by fellow Jews as part of an age-old pattern of rebellion against God. They had "killed the Lord Jesus." Before that, they had murdered the "prophets." They had driven out Paul and his associates.

The result of the opposition of the Jews to the advance of the gospel was that "they always heap up their sins to the limit." Commenting on this phrase, A. T. Robertson said, "It may be God's conceived plan to allow the Jews to go on and fill up (fill up full), or it may be the natural result from the continual sins of the Jews" (*Word Pictures in the New Testament*, vol. 4, p. 22).

"Encouraging, comforting, urging"

These verbs indicate the act of encouraging or cheering someone. "Encouraging" more frequently than "comforting" carries the idea of exhortation; yet both are also used in contexts of admonition. The combination of those two verbs in Paul's writings seems to indicate a positive encouragement to Christian living. "Urging" speaks of the delivery of truth and is likely intended to convey the more directive functions of a father.

Acts recounts the intense Jewish hostility to the gospel in Thessalonica (Acts 17:1ff.). The situation deteriorated to such an extent that the Thessalonian believers ushered the missionaries out of the city by night.

We are not sure what Paul meant by his last statement in verse 16. It is perhaps the most difficult statement in the passage. "God's wrath" in Paul's thought usually referred to the outpouring of His wrath at the end of this age. Here, however, it seems to refer to some occurrence or experience that Paul interpreted to mean that God's wrath had overtaken the rebellious Jews at last.

■ *After receiving the gospel, the Thessalonian*
■ *believers endured intense persecution. Paul*
■ *expressed his deep concern and exasperation*
■ *with his countrymen. Their rejection of the*
■ *gospel moved Paul to bitter denunciation*
■ *similiar to the Old Testament prophets.*

PAUL'S DESIRE TO VISIT THE CHURCH (2:17–20)

From Paul's comments about his departure, we see how much he wanted to stay. Evidently, he feared that the Thessalonians were not strong enough to confront the hostility toward their new faith. Paul used emotionally charged language to describe his separation and absence from the church. Paul said that the missionaries were "torn away" from the church. The word Paul used here means literally "orphaned." The strong bond between Paul and the church, comparable to the bond between loving parent and beloved child, made separation emotionally painful for the apostle. Paul's description of his separation was designed to express clearly that his absence did not result from indifference on his part.

Paul made repeated attempts to return to Thessalonica, but Satan thwarted his efforts. Sometimes Paul saw obstacles and problems as expressing the will of God (Rom. 1:13). In this case, they expressed Satan's opposition to God.

How important were the Thessalonians to Paul? He made every effort to let them know that they were absolutely indispensable. They were his "glory" and "joy," both in the present as well as at the future coming of Christ.

- Paul longed to see the Thessalonians again
- with the joyful anticipation similar to that of
- parents eager to look upon their firstborn.

"When He comes"

This phrase translates The New Testament word *parousia.* It denotes the manifestation of a deity or the visit of a king or emperor. Early Christians used this phrase to refer to the coming of Jesus in power and glory at the end of the age.

QUESTIONS TO GUIDE YOUR STUDY

1. What are some ways the missionaries asserted their love for the believers at Thessalonica?

2. In defending the motives of his ministry with the Thessalonians, on what basis did Paul do so?

3. In describing his relationship with the Thessalonians, Paul used the analogies of a nursing mother (vv. 6–8) and a father (vv. 9–10). In what ways did he function as both toward the Thessalonians?

4. Paul greatly desired to visit the Thessalonians. What was his motivation? Why had he been prevented from returning to the church?

The Acts account offers little insight at this point. There we are told that Jewish opposition drove Paul from Thessalonica to Berea and then to Athens (Acts 17:1–5). Acts 17:14–15 indicates that Timothy and Silas stayed in Berea when Paul fled to Athens, but they were expected to join Paul in Athens as soon as possible.

We get a view into Paul's heart in this chapter of 1 Thessalonians. He expressed his deepest concerns for the church. He needed to know how the Thessalonians were doing in the midst of persecution.

THE DECISION TO SEND TIMOTHY (3:1–5)

Unable to make the desired visit to Thessalonica personally, Paul's anxiety about the new converts there became unbearable. In this situation he decided to send Timothy back to visit them, even though it meant he had to remain in Athens without his trusted friend.

Paul's reason for sending Timothy to visit the Thessalonians is clear. The Thessalonians were under great pressure from their adversaries. Timothy was to perform the pastoral function of encouraging and exhorting the believers to remain true to Jesus Christ in spite of persecution. Paul knew that the "lot" of believers is persecution, such as the Thessalonians were experiencing.

Paul used three infinitives to explain Timothy's mission as highlighted in the following chart:

Timothy's Mission to the Thessalonians

Ministry Directives	Desired Result
1. To strengthen them in the faith	That the Thessalonians might remain true to Christ.
2. To encourage them in the faith	Same as above.
3. To prevent them from being "unsettled" by affliction	That the Thessalonians might resist being discouraged by affliction.

Verse 5 reveals why Paul was anxious for the Thessalonians. He wants to find out about their faith—that is, if their trust in Jesus was of the quality that could stand up under persecution. Also, he wanted to feel that he had engaged in useful and lasting labor with regard to the Thessalonian church.

"Tempter" is another name for Satan. The believers at Thessalonica faced both temptation (v. 3) and affliction (v. 5). What is the temptation in the time of opposition and suffering? It comes from the sense that we have been abandoned by God. Suffering can also lead us to believe that our trust is absurd. If the Thessalonians had renounced their faith in the midst of their persecution, Paul would have considered his labor with the Thessalonians as fruitless.

Timothy, whose name means "honoring God," was a friend and trusted coworker of Paul. When Timothy was a child, his mother Eunice and his grandmother Lois taught him the Scriptures (2 Tim. 1:5; 3:15). A native of Lystra, he may have been converted on Paul's first missionary journey (Acts 14:6–23). Paul referred to Timothy as his child in the faith. (1 Cor. 4:17; 1 Tim. 1:2; 2 Tim. 1:2). This probably means that Paul was instrumental in Timothy's conversion.

■ *Paul sent Timothy to visit the believers at*
■ *Thessalonica. He was anxious about them*
■ *and wanted to know that the church had per-*
■ *sisted in its commitment to Jesus Christ. In*
■ *addition, he wanted to feel that he had*
■ *engaged in useful and lasting labor.*

TIMOTHY RETURNS WITH GOOD NEWS (3:6–10)

Timothy returned from his mission to the Thessalonians with the kind of report that Paul had hoped to hear. Timothy's good news encouraged the missionaries. Overjoyed by the news from the little band of besieged Christians, Paul decides to communicate with them by letter. His enthusiasm was conveyed by the speed with which he responded to the news. "Timothy has

"Standing firm"

This verb means "to stand firm, to be steadfast." It is used repeatedly in the New Testament as a call for continued perseverance. The Thessalonian believers were persevering in godliness in the midst of affliction. Other New Testament uses of this word include "persevering" in the faith (1 Cor. 16:13); in the Spirit (Phil. 1:27); in one's fellowship with the Lord (Phil. 4:1); and in Christian freedom (Gal. 5:1).

come just now" implies that Paul was making his response a high priority.

The good news Timothy brought was twofold:

1. He told about the "faith and love" of the Christian community at Thessalonica. The Thessalonians had trusted God, and they had not abandoned this trust under pressure.

2. Timothy also reported that the Thessalonians always remembered their missionaries with respect and love. They shared Paul's desire for a reunion.

The phrase "since you are standing firm" (NIV) suggests certainty, and it sounds like a statement about past perseverance. The sentence, however, is conditional and might better be rendered "if you stand fast" (RSV), implying a future expectation rather than a statement about the past.

"What is lacking" (v. 10) may refer to a natural growth toward completion or, more negatively, a deficiency or inadequacy that needed to be corrected. In none of Paul's letters do we get the idea that Christians in the churches had arrived at the zenith of their development. No matter what their progress, there was always room for further development.

■ *Timothy's encouraging report of the favor-*
■ *able feelings of the Thessalonians toward*
■ *Paul—and the fact that they had trusted God*
■ *and not abandoned that trust under pres-*
■ *sure—were reasons for joy.*

PAUL'S PRAYER (3:11–13)

Paul concluded this first major section of his letter with a prayer. The apostle addressed three requests to God: (1) He wanted God to "clear the way" for his visit to Thessalonica; (2) he wanted God to cause their love to overflow; and (3) he asked God to "strengthen" their "hearts."

"Clear the Way" (v. 11)

Paul's first request was that God would "clear the way" for his personal visit to the church.

"Make Your Love Increase and Overflow" (v. 12)

Paul's second prayer petition is that the Lord might cause the believers to "increase and overflow" in their love for others. Together those two words form an emphatic prayer-wish for the spiritual growth of the Thessalonians. This love was not exclusive; it is expressed to "each other" and "everyone else."

"Strengthen Your Hearts" (v. 13)

The heart is the center of the intellect and will. Paul in this verse referred to resolution and commitment. Paul's goal for requesting that God strengthen the hearts of the Thessalonians was that they be "blameless and holy" in the presence of God. God's saints, or holy ones, are those dedicated to Him and His service. He wants them to be strengthened in their dedication to a holy life—one completely devoted to God.

The word translated "clear the way" can mean "to straighten out, to make straight" or simply "to direct." The former would imply the need to remove obstacles, and it seems more likely to be Paul's intent in this context. Some spiritual hindrance had kept them from visiting the Thessalonians: "Satan stopped us" (2:18). Spiritual power is required to remove a spiritual hindrance. According to travels recorded in Acts, Paul's visit to Thessalonica did not happen for several years, not until after the Ephesian ministry (20:1–6).

N

- Paul's prayer reflected the transition in his
- life from anguish to exhilaration. He prayed
- that God would enable him to visit his
- friends. He then asked God to perfect and
- enlarge the love which the Thessalonians
- had already displayed toward one another.

QUESTIONS TO GUIDE YOUR STUDY

1. Why did Paul send Timothy to the Thessalonians? And what specifically was his mission?
2. What was the content of Timothy's report to Paul about the Thessalonians?
3. Timothy reported that the Thessalonians were "standing firm in the Lord." Given their circumstances, what did that mean?
4. Describe the petitions of Paul's prayer in verses 11–13. What was the occasion for the prayer? What was the goal of his prayer?

Paul could have ended his letter with chapter 3, for he had discussed the most important concern on his mind. Instead, he added to the letter a second section that contains ethical appeals and instructions. Some of these subjects probably were suggested by Timothy's good report from Thessalonica.

AN INTRODUCTORY CALL TO OBEDIENCE (4:1–2)

Paul began this section by appealing to the Thessalonians. "Ask" and "urge" are synonyms. They come after "finally, brothers" in the original Greek text, providing a sense of urgency to Paul's words and creating anticipation on the part of the readers.

"In the Lord Jesus" describes the context of his appeal. Jesus was Lord of Paul's life and theirs. The apostle had given the Thessalonians instructions about Christian behavior—how they were to live and "to please God." He diplomatically affirmed that the Thessalonians were indeed following those instructions. Yet there was room for development and growth, so Paul urged them to do "more and more." His challenges to continue in Christian growth, however, did not minimize the progress his readers had already made toward living out the implications of the gospel.

Paul used two comparative clauses (introduced by the phrase *as*) to express what the Thessalonians were to do. "We ask and urge you in the Lord Jesus that, *as* you learned from us how you ought to live and to please God (*as*, in fact,

"How to live" and "you are living"

The words of this phrase translate the verb that means "walk." Forms of this word occur twice in 1 Thess. 4:1, and they are translated "live" and "living." Both refer to behavior or conduct. "Paul is fond of the metaphor 'walk' (*peripeteo*).

A. T. Robertson, *Word Pictures in the New Testament*, vol. 4, 410.

you are doing), you should do more" (NRSV, italics added).

This instruction guided the new believers in how they were "to live" and "to please God." Paul used the present tense with both of these infinitives to imply that consistent behavior was expected—and not just the occasional acts of obedience.

Continuing to live in a way that pleased God did not require the return of the apostle or the revelation of new traditions. It required obedience to the commands the church had already received. It also required obedience to the commands of Jesus. The verses that followed provided some specific content in places where Paul apparently felt the Thessalonians needed clarification or encouragement.

- *Continuing to live in a way that pleased God*
- *required obedience to the commands of Jesus.*
- *Paul instructed the Thessalonians to continue in their Christian growth.*

EXHORTATIONS ABOUT SANCTIFICATION (4:3–8)

Holiness in the Sexual Life (vv. 3–6a)

This first of several exhortations began with the statement that what follows is "God's will." The theme of this section is a call to *sanctification*. The specific commands in verses 3b–6 are examples of sanctified living in regard to sexual purity.

Paul made it very clear in his letters that high moral standards were important to the Christian life. If believers are to be holy, certain practices

Sanctification

Sanctification is the gradual process of being made holy, of being set apart for God, resulting in a changed lifestyle for the believer. This process takes the believer through failure because of self-dependency to triumph through the indwelling Spirit. What does it mean to live a sanctified life? At its basic level, it means living in a manner consistent with the character and commands of God.

must be rejected. In this context, Paul high-lighted three aspects of sanctification. One who is sanctified:

- Should avoid sexual immorality (v. 3)
- Should know how to control his or her own body (vv. 4–5)
- Should not "wrong a brother or take advantage of him" (v. 6)

A Solemn Warning (vv. 6b–8)

These verses present a fourfold warning. They are not directed to the pagan but to those members of the church who choose to live in a manner that denies the God they claim to serve. Paul gave four reasons why Christians should adhere to a life of moral purity.

1. *God will punish sinful behavior* (v. 6b). Salvation does not grant believers the right to sin without suffering the consequences.
2. *Sexual sins are inconsistent with the sanctified life* (v. 7). The "call" Paul referred to seems to look back at their initial commitment to follow Christ. The nature of the Thessalonians' call and the purpose to which He called them require not impurity but sanctification.
3. *He who rejects this instruction rejects God* (v. 8a). Because God calls believers to a sanctified life rather than immoral behavior, living immorally is a rejection of God. Rejection indicates a settled attitude, not a single incident of disobedience.
4. *Living an unsanctified life is inconsistent with the character of the Holy Spirit, who indwells the believer* (v. 8b). To live an immoral lifestyle is to reject God's gift of

the Spirit. The work of the Holy Spirit must be evident in the sanctified living of believers (Gal. 5:16–26). This is the will of God for His people. To live immorally is to deny the presence of the Spirit.

■ *The prevailing sexual laxity that Paul wit-*
■ *nessed throughout the Roman Empire com-*
■ *pelled him to remind his readers that sexual*
■ *purity was the will of God. Anyone who vio-*
■ *lated God's standards at this point faced cer-*
■ *tain punishment from the Lord. Paul made it*
■ *clear that God had not called believers to a*
■ *life of impurity but a life of holiness.*

EXHORTATIONS ABOUT BROTHERLY LOVE (4:9–12)

In his exhortations to the churches to which he ministered, Paul usually put love and unity in the community ahead of his call for personal morality. In this section he reversed the order and turned to the matter of love after talking about the need for sexual purity.

Love among Brothers (vv. 9–10)

Paul's theme for these two verses was love for fellow Christians, whereas he dealt with the theme of relating to non-Christian society in verses 11–12.

Paul's only directive in this passage was "we urge you." He expanded this directive with a series of suggested actions that would allow the Thessalonians to excel on a path that leads to the final, intended outcome.

The love of the Thessalonian congregation was to include "all the brothers throughout Macedonia." We may assume that their love was

"Brotherly love"

The phrase "brotherly love" (the Greek word, *philadelphias*) is a translation of a word that is made up of two words: "love" and "brother." Outside of the New Testament, both Greek and Jewish writers used "brotherly Love" primarily of love within actual families, not of love within religious groups. In the New Testament, however, it is always used as it is here—of love between members of the Christian family (Rom. 12:10; Heb. 13:1; 1 Pet. 1:22; 2 Pet. 1:7).

Paul's Exhortations to Brotherly Love

ACTION:	VERSE
Love the brothers even more	v. 10*b*
Aspire to lead a quiet life	v. 11
Mind their own affairs	v. 11
Work with their own hands	v. 11
Goals:	
1. To "win the respect of outsiders."	
2. To "not be dependent on anybody."	v. 12

lived out in concrete ministry to the needs of other Christians. We get some notion of this spirit of the Macedonian believers when we read 2 Cor. 8:1–5.

Paul urged the Thessalonians to love the brothers "more and more." No Christian reaches the zenith of such love in his or her spiritual life in this world.

Conduct in the Community (vv. 11–12)

Paul moved naturally from relationships in the church to the Christian's conduct in society. The believer's manner of life should be the kind that would earn respect from unbelieving neighbors.

Christians in the first century were often found in the center of trouble and disorder because of preaching the gospel. Paul himself had that experience. But he did not believe Christians should get into trouble because of disorderly conduct, interference in other people's business, or failure to earn a living.

■ *God's will for believers includes moral purity*
■ *and love relationships with people, which*
■ *demands openness and self-sacrifice.*

EXHORTATIONS REGARDING THOSE WHO HAVE ALREADY DIED (4:13–18)

"Do Not . . . Be Ignorant" (vv. 13–14)

Apparently, early Christians expected the Lord would return before they died. In Thessalonica, some of the believers had already died. The church evidently had some questions about this. What would happen to their brothers and sisters who were not alive when Jesus appeared? In this passage Paul answered that question.

For Paul the future of believers after death was tied to the resurrection of Jesus Christ. Christians believed that God had raised Jesus from the dead. They needed to be confident also that the relationship of believers to God in Christ did not end with death. The physical death of Christians, however, presented no problem to the God who brought Jesus back from the dead.

Those Who Are Alive Will "Not Precede Those Who Have Fallen Asleep" (vv. 15–18)

Verses 15–17 describe the scenario of the end-time. The main point in the passage was Paul's insistence that being alive at the return of the Lord would give no advantage to his readers. They would not "precede those who have fallen asleep."

Paul made two primary statements in verse 16 and one in verse 17; these provide the core sequence of events regarding Jesus' coming. Three key events constitute Paul's vision of Jesus' return: (1) The Lord will appear (16a); (2) the "dead in Christ" will be raised (16b); and (3) all believers will be caught up to "meet the Lord in the air" (v. 17). The following chart depicts the sequence and details of these events.

The Lord's Return (The Rapture)

Event	Verse	Details of the Event
1. Appearing of the Lord	v. 16a	• the Lord will come down from heaven → with a loud command → with the voice of the archangel → with the trumpet call of God
2. Raising of the "dead in Christ"	v. 16b	• the dead will rise first
3. Believers "caught up"	v. 17	• together with the "dead in Christ" → in the clouds → to meet the Lord in the air

Living believers are said to be "caught up" to meet the Lord at His coming. But this is not understood in the same way by all interpreters. Those of varying millennial views about the end-time events all hold firmly to the biblical truth of such a rapture. However, it is within the premillenial view that the teaching of the rapture finds major emphasis. This view sees a tribulation period immediately before the Second Coming of Christ. Postmillennial and amillennial perspectives generally understand the rapture as a part of the Day of the Lord when Jesus will return to gather His people to Himself.

The period of tribulation mentioned above is referred to as the Great Tribulation. It is a seven-year period of intense trouble on earth prior to the Second Coming of Christ. There are three basic views regarding the tribulation, as explained in the chart on the following page.

The "Rapture"

The event described in verses 16–17, commonly referred to as the "rapture," holds a prominent place in the study of the last days. It refers to the catching up of believers by Christ at the time of His return.

Views of the Tribulation

VIEW	EXPLANATION
Pretribulational	Sees the rapture occurring prior to the tribulation.
Midtribulational	Places the rapture at the midpoint of a seven-year tribulation period.
Posttribulational	Holds that the church will remain on earth during the tribulation period.*

*For more information on the Lord's return, see the article, "The Return of Christ" at the back of this book.

- *The believing community should not grieve*
- *over those who have died in Jesus, for God*
- *will bring them with Jesus at the return of the*
- *Lord. At the Lord's appearing, the Christian*
- *dead will be raised to meet the Lord in the air*
- *together with those have been "caught up"*
- *(who are alive and remaining). Paul*
- *exhorted believers to comfort one another*
- *with these words.*

Paul wanted his readers to believe that physical death was no problem for believers, so he closed this section with the command to "encourage each other" with these words. Just as the Thessalonians were called to comfort one another, so believers of every age are called to "rejoice with those who rejoice" and "mourn with those who mourn." This is Paul's message of comfort.

QUESTIONS TO GUIDE YOUR STUDY

1. What was the point of Paul's introductory call to obedience at the beginning of this chapter?

2. What is the doctrine of sanctification? What did Paul teach about holiness in the sexual life?

3. Paul exhorted the Thessalonians to "brotherly love." How might we apply his exhortation to the modern-day church?

4. What does the term *rapture* mean? What events does Paul describe regarding the Lord's return? What should be the believer's attitude toward the Lord's return?

This chapter contains two major sections. In the first, Paul continued his discussion about the Lord's return with an emphasis on the Day of the Lord. The concluding section emphasized responsibilities to the different people in the Christian community.

THE DAY OF THE LORD (5:1–11)

This section continues Paul's discussion of the Lord's coming from chapter 4, but with this section he changed his emphasis. Whereas 4:13–18 addressed the concerns regarding believers who had already died, these verses addressed the responsibility of living believers as they await the Lord's return.

The Thessalonians' Question (v. 1)

When is the Lord going to return? is a question that has been on the minds of believers for centuries. Paul's response to a specific time was: "About times and dates we do not need to write to you." He did, however, remind the Thessalonians that the Lord's return is inevitable and will surprise unbelievers. In contrast to unbelievers, believers need to remain alert and watchful for His return.

Descriptions of the Lord's Return (vv. 2–3)

Paul used two analogies to describe the manner of the Lord's return:

Its unexpectedness. The Lord will come "like a thief in the night." A thief does not announce his coming, so the specific time of his arrival is unknown. Only those who are unbelievers, however, will be taken by surprise.

Day of the Lord

The phrase "Day of the Lord" is full of meaning to anyone familiar with the Jewish Scriptures. In the Old Testament, it is a day of judgment. Yahweh will punish the evil within Israel (Amos 5:18–20) on that day, and the wicked among the nations will face a day of terrible wrath (Isa. 13:6–13; Obad. 15), Those who have not repented will face "destruction from the Almighty" (Joel 1:13–15). Yet the punishment of the evil is at the same time the deliverance of the righteous (Joel 2:31–32; Zech. 14:1–21; Mal. 4:5). In the New Testament, Jesus is the Lord whom God has appointed to judge the world (Acts 17:31), so the day of the Lord (2 Thess. 2:2; 1 Cor. 5:5; 2 Pet. 3:10) is the day of the Lord Jesus Christ (1 Cor. 1:8; 2 Cor. 1:14; Phil. 1:6–10; 2:16).

Its suddenness. Its suddenness will be like the onslaught of labor pains which a pregnant woman experiences. In addition, when a pregnant woman actually begins labor, there is no "escape" (v. 3). Its conclusion is inevitable.

Anticipating the Return (vv. 4–11)

How should believers live in light of the Lord's return? Paul provided additional instruction to address this question. Believers should prepare for the Lord's return by disciplined, godly living supported by hope, love, and faith. Watching for Jesus' return involves consistent living in obedience to the Lord's commands. Paul gave his readers these exhortations:

1. *"Let us be alert."* The word *alert* means to stay awake. Believers need to be like a watchman that never falls asleep at his post.

2. *"Let us be . . . self-controlled."* This is a word that means "to be calm, sober-minded" (see A. T. Robertson, *Word Pictures in the New Testament*, vol. 4, 35). A person like this is aware of what is happening around him.

The believer is to be alert, similiar to a soldier putting on armor. The Christian soldier's armor includes those qualities and attributes already in the believer's possession: (1) The "breastplate" of love and faith; and (2) the "helmet" of the hope of salvation.

Paul closed this section by admonishing his readers to encourage one another with these truths about the Lord's return. Believers should encourage and build up one another in the faith, knowing that one day they will live with Christ.

- *Because the Day of the Lord will come sud-*
- *denly and unexpectedly, bringing destruction*
- *on those who are spiritually insensitive,*
- *believers should maintain spiritual alertness.*

CONCLUDING EXHORTATIONS (5:12–22)

This concluding section emphasized the church's responsibilities to different people within the Christian community.

Leaders and Followers (vv. 12–13)

Leaders are to respect those who follow their leadership. Paul identified three areas associated with this relationship between the leaders and followers:

1. *Those who work hard* (v. 12). These were laborers who worked hard in the work of the ministry so as to earn the respect of the congregation.

2. *Those who are over you* (v. 12). These were individuals who directed or cared for others in the church.

3. *Those who admonish you* (v. 12). These were leaders or members of the congregation who admonished one another to proper behavior.

Paul exhorted the congregation at Thessalonica to acknowledge and respect those who were ministering in their midst. They were to "live in peace with each other" (v. 13).

The Weak and the Strong (vv. 14–15)

In verse 14 Paul provided four brief exhortations for the church ("brothers" refers to the entire congregation) that encouraged it to take

"Destruction"

What is the "sudden destruction" that comes upon the unbeliever? This destruction at the end is sudden, but it is surprise—not speed—that is the point. In 2 Thess. 1:8–9, Paul proclaimed the everlasting "destruction" of "those who do not know God and do not obey the gospel." Those who refuse to acknowledge or obey God live in a self-imposed ignorance. They are ignorant not only of the God who is but also of the God who will judge them. Their moment of judgment will come as a shock.

There will be no delay, no opportunity to take care of neglected business. There will be no second chance, no opportunity for additional preparation before meeting the Lord.

D. Michael Martin, *1, 2 Thessalonians,* (NAC), 160–61.

"Idle" or "Unruly"

The Greek word behind these translations is a military term that describes soldiers who don't keep in the ranks.

Leon Morris, *The Epistles of Paul to the Thessalonians*, (Grand Rapids: Eerdmans, 1958), 100.

"Henri Nouwen's image of the wounded healer is a model for the church's ministry to the weak. The man sits at the gate with the other sick and diseased. His wounds are just as deep; his suffering is just as severe as others who live the life of hurt. But he takes time out from dressing his own wounds to clean and bandage the wounds of others."

John D. Hendrix, *To Thessalonians with Love* (Nashville: Broaman, 1982), 116.

protective measures to assist troublesome or weak Christians:

1. *"Warn those who are idle."* Those who were idle had entered into an unacceptable lifestyle and they needed to be confronted about their behavior.

2. *"Encourage the timid."* Those who were "faint-hearted" or discouraged by their circumstances or a turn of events needed to be encouraged.

3. *"Help the weak."* This can refer to those who were physically weak or ill as well as those who were spiritually weak or immature. The church was to support these weak members and not desert them.

4. *"Be patient with everyone."* Patience is a characteristic of God. The believers at Thessalonica were to demonstrate godly patience in dealing with troublesome members, just as God had demonstrated His patience in their lives.

Optimists and Pessimists (vv. 16–18)

These three brief exhortations commend joyful worship directed toward God and should be evident in all assemblies where Christians gather for worship:

1. *"Be joyful"* (v. 16). Joy is a work produced in the believer by the Spirit. The believer who is joyful rejoices in the good fortune of others and is obedient to the Lord.

2. *"Pray continually"* (v. 17). "God is with us whatever befalls us. It is God's will that we find joy in prayer in Christ Jesus in every condition of life" (A. T. Robertson, *Word Pictures in the New Testament*, vol. 4, p. 37).

3. *"Give thanks in all circumstances"* (v. 18). Believers should constantly give thanks to God for what He has done in their lives. Paul was particularly thankful for what God had done in the Thessalonian church.

The Cynical and the Gullible (vv. 19–22)

Paul wrote this group of five exhortations to help the Thessalonians hold their ground in the midst of conflicting claims about truth:

1. *"Do not put out the Spirit's fire"* (v. 19). The New Testament uses fire as a symbol for the Spirit. This exhortation is a prohibition that forbids the Thessalonians from suppressing or stifling the work of the Spirit in their church. The following exhortation provided an example of putting out the Spirit's fire.

2. *"Do not treat prophecies with contempt"* (v. 20). Those with the gift of prophecy proclaimed the word of God to the congregation. The congregation might "put out the Spirit's fire" by refusing to hear the word of the prophet.

3. *"Test everything. Hold on to the good"* (v. 21). To "test" something is to examine it carefully. This included the church carefully examining the teaching of visiting teachers and prophets as well as its own members and leaders. What proved to be "good" they were to retain and allow it to shape their lives.

4. *"Avoid every kind of evil"* (v. 22). "Kind of evil" is a translation of a word that means "look" or "appearance." Upon careful testing, whatever appeared evil Paul called on the church to avoid. "Evil had a way of showing itself even in the spiritual

"Modern discussions generally insist that a prophet's function was rather to 'forth-tell' than to 'fore-tell.' While there is truth in this it should not be forgotten that on occasion the prophet would foretell the future."

Leon Morris,
The First and Second Epistles to the Thessalonians
(Grand Rapids: Eerdmans, 1959), 176–177.

"Test," "Prove"

These terms are "often used in testing metals or checking out budgets. 'Prove all things' (KJV) refers to the process of sifting out the genuine from the counterfeit. Paul was not saying to try everything once. He was saying that we should test everthing that represents itself as good. The good should be accepted. Every kind of evil should be avoided."

John D. Hendrix, *To Thessalonians with Love* (Nashville: Broaman, 1982), 122–123.

gifts including prophecy" (A. T. Robertson, *Word Pictures in the New Testament*, vol. 4, p. 38).

■ *In this section Paul reflected on the church's*
■ *responsibilities to different people within the*
■ *Christian community. With a series of brief*
■ *exhortations, he urged the church members*
■ *to embrace one another as well as the com-*
■ *munity in ways that honor and glorify God.*

BENEDICTION AND CONCLUSION (5:23–28)

Benediction (vv. 23–24)

Paul concluded his letter with a prayer that highlights two of the key themes of the letter. His first prayer request was that God might sanctify the Thessalonians, "through and through." His second request was for the preservation of the church.

Paul concluded his prayer by assuring the Thessalonians that God is faithful and will do what He promises. Paul left his readers with the assurances that those who are in Christ will be sanctified and kept, making their future secure.

Concluding Remarks (vv. 25–27)

Following his prayer for the Thessalonian congregation, Paul presented them with three brief exhortations:

1. *"Pray for us."* Paul pleaded for the prayers of his converts at Thessalonica. Paul used the present tense, which indicated that he wanted them to "pray continually."

2. *"Greet all brothers with a holy kiss."* The holy kiss was widely practiced among the

early Christians as a greeting, a sign of acceptance, and as an impartation of blessing. This custom may have been used to express the unity of Christian fellowship.

3. *"I charge you . . . to have this letter read."* According to A. T. Robertson, the word "charge" means "to put one to oath" (*Word Pictures in the New Testament*, vol. 4, p. 39). Paul was requiring a pledge from the Thessalonians that they would read his letter "to all the brothers."

Conclusion of the Letter (v. 28)

The typical closing to an ancient letter was a simple "farewell." Paul replaced the secular formula with a benediction. Paul's signature theme—the grace of the Lord Jesus Christ—concluded this letter. He reminded his readers that Jesus Christ is the source of God's grace then applied that grace to his readers.

"Many people could not read, so reading his letter aloud was the only way everyone in the congregation could be acquainted with it."

Craig S. Keener, *The IVP Bible Background Commentary* (Downers Grove: InterVarsity Press, 1993), 596.

■ *Paul offered edifying words of assurance and*
■ *blessing for the church. These comments*
■ *underscore the importance of prayer in car-*
■ *rying out the purposes of God.*

QUESTIONS TO GUIDE YOUR STUDY

1. How did Paul respond to questions about the time of the Lord's return? Is it really necessary that we know when His return will be?

2. What is the "Day of the Lord"? What does it mean to believers? to unbelievers?

3. How should believers live in anticipation of the Lord's return?

4. Paul gave several concluding exhortations to the church at Thessalonica regarding its responsibilities to different people within the Christian community. Do any of these apply to your church?

Paul wrote this letter to the Thessalonians to deal with three major issues. First, there was the matter of continued persecution to which the church was still subjected and which it apparently continued to meet with courage and faithfulness. Second, some person or persons had proclaimed to the church that the Day of the Lord had already come. Third, some members of the church were guilty of idleness and disorderly conduct.

In this first chapter, Paul emphasized the dire consequences that awaited the persecutors of the Thessalonians through the judgment of God.

THE SALUTATION (1:1–2)

Authors (v. 1a)

As with 1 Thessalonians, the three men involved in the writing of the letter were Paul, Silas, and Timothy. (See 1 Thess. 1:1 for information about these men.)

Recipients (v. 1b)

Here, as in all his letters, Paul followed the conventional Hellenistic form of address. Although he followed this form, he did so with a distinctly Christian flair.

Greeting (v. 2)

The greeting of 2 Thessalonians is identical to that in 1 Thessalonians except for the addition of the pronoun *our* in the first verse and the phrase "from God our Father and the Lord Jesus Christ (v. 2). (See 1 Thess. 1:1 for a discussion of the terms *grace* and *peace*.) God's gracious act

The Hellenistic Letter

Generally, Paul's epistles seem to follow the normal pattern of the Hellenistic letter, which consists of five major sections:

1. Opening (sender, addressee, greeting)

2. Thanksgiving or blessing (often with a prayer of intercession, well wishes, or personal greetings)

3. The burden of the letter (including citation of classical sources and arguments)

4. *Parenesis* (ethical instruction, exhortation)

5. Closing (mention of personal plans, mutual friends, benediction)

in Christ and the well-being that can result is the basic tenet of the Christian faith.

Paul used the term *Father* as his first designation of God. This title reminded his readers that a relationship exists not only between the father and His children, but also between the siblings. Children who share the same Father are bound together in a single family and should demonstrate love and concern for one another.

- The second letter to the Thessalonians begins
- by identifying Paul, Silas, and Timothy as its
- senders. No doubt, Paul was the primary
- author. The letter's beginning follows the
- pattern of most of Paul's letters.

PAUL'S GRATITUDE FOR THE BELIEVERS (1:3–4)

Before turning to the problems in the churches to which he wrote, Paul usually expressed thanksgiving for the good things in their lives. He did the same here, but with a different twist. His expressions of thanksgiving, here and in 2 Thess. 2:13, are unusual in that they included a sense of obligation. "We ought" implies that the giving of thanks was not an option. He also expressed that thanksgiving was "fitting," which emphasized further the Christian sense of moral obligation.

Why did Paul use these expressions? Some interpreters suggest that the Thessalonians had protested their unworthiness of Paul's praise in the previous letter. Where "faith" and "love" existed in the church, however, it was wrong not to be grateful to God who was their source.

"Growing" faith and "increasing" love were cause for Paul's thanksgiving in this letter. Faith and love are not static; they are dynamic. We can never trust or love as much we ought, so we need to be concerned about increasing these as well as their presence.

Christian Dynamics at Work in Thessalonica

VIRTUE	DYNAMIC AT WORK	DIRECTED TOWARD
Faith	"growing more and more"	God
Love	"increasing"	Other believers

Paul continued his thanksgiving by saying that the growing faith and increasing love of the church were cause for boasting. Paul boasted partly because the Thessalonians' faith and love were growing in spite of persecution.

Paul's emphasis on this boast before other congregations served two purposes: (1) It intensified the affirmation; and (2) it implied that the Thessalonians had a reputation to live up to, thus encouraging continued perseverance.

- Paul commended the Thessalonians for their
- growing faith and their maturing love and
- patience. They became the object of his
- boasting to other congregations.

"Boast"

The word *boast* means "to make a boast of, take pride in." In all the New Testament, it is used only here. Its compounded form ("in" + "boast" = "to boast in") gives it more emphasis than the uncompounded form ("boast") that Paul frequently used.

"Paul was not above praising one church to other churches to provoke them to good works. Here he is boasting of Thessalonica in Macedonia to the Corinthians as he did later to the Corinthians about the collection (2 Cor. 8:1–15) after first boasting to the Macedonians about the Corinthians (2 Cor. 9:1–5)."

A. T. Robertson, *Word Pictures in the New Testament*, vol. 4, 42.

THE OUTCOME OF PERSEVERANCE (1:5–10)

These verses are an elaboration that addressed one of the great hopes the apostle had for the church—that they would persevere. Paul encouraged the Thessalonians' perseverance by pointing out its end result as well as the end result of opposition to faith. Because God is just, He will ultimately reward the faithful and punish the wicked.

The Perseverance of the Thessalonians (v. 5)

It is difficult to determine what exactly Paul considered to be "evidence that God's judgment is right." It could have been both the fact that they are suffering and that they are bearing up under their suffering. Today, this is evidence of God's presence in the church. The power of God in the life of the believers was proof that they would emerge victorious.

Evil had not prevailed. The enemy could not accomplish his purpose. This was evidence of the weakness of the forces opposed to God. Perseverance in persecution meant that God would count the Thessalonians "worthy of the kingdom of God" (that is, in His victorious rule).

God's Righteous Vindication (vv. 6–10)

Vindication of the persecuted is one aspect of the righteousness of God's judgment. The other aspect is the punishment that will be meted out to the persecutors. The just judgment of God will "pay back" afflictors with affliction and give rest to the afflicted (v. 7). "It is mine to avenge, I will repay, says the Lord" (Isa. 66:6). In the context of the unjust suffering of the righteous at the hands of the unrighteous, this promise is an assurance that evil persons ultimately will received the punishment they deserve.

"The New Testament does not look on suffering in quite the same way as do most modern people. To us it is in itself an evil, something to be avoided at all costs. Now while the New Testament does not gloss over this aspect of suffering, it does not lose sight either of the fact that in the good providence of God suffering is often the means of working out God's eternal purpose. It develops in the sufferers qualities of character."

Leon Morris
The First and Second Epistles to the Thessalonians (Grand Rapids: Eerdmans, 1959), 197.

Words for Suffering

TERM	MEANING	EXAMPLES	CROSS-REFERENCES
"Persecutions"	Especially religious persecutions	Political opposition to the preaching of the gospel; physical violence, such as stoning	Rom. 8:35; 2 Tim. 3:11
"Trials"	Pressure; metaphorically, some burdensome or chafing oppression	Pressure of circumstances; antagonism of persons	1 Thess. 1:6; 3:3, 7

The promise of balancing accounts in the future will not remove suffering from believers, but it does help them put suffering in perspective.

Just as persecutors will be punished for inflicting suffering on the righteous, faithful believers can anticipate God's rest ("relief," v. 7) in the glorious kingdom of the Lord Jesus.

- *In the coming judgment, God will reverse the*
- *present roles of the persecuted and the perse-*
- *cutors. God's people can be encouraged by*
- *knowing that they will be vindicated at the*
- *Lord's coming and will realize they have nei-*
- *ther believed nor suffered in vain.*

PAUL'S PRAYER FOR THE THESSALONIANS (1:11–12)

Paul was always conscious that the future of believers was dependent on God. Therefore, it was not at all contradictory for him to assure his

"Rest"

The word Paul used to indicate *relief* originally meant the release of the tension on a bowstring. According to A. T. Robertson, rest means "let up, release . . . from troubles here (2 Cor. 2:13; 7:5; 8:13), and hereafter. Vivid word. They shared suffering with Paul (v. 5) and so will share the *rest*."

A.T. Robertson, *Word Pictures in the New Testament*, vol. 4, 43.

"Work of Faith"

"Paul prays for rich fruition of what he had seen in the beginning. Work marked by faith, springs from faith, sustained by faith."

A.T. Robertson, *Word Pictures in the New Testament*, vol. 4, 45–46.

readers that God would count them worthy and at the same time constantly pray to God that He would do so.

"Every act prompted by your faith" should be understood as the resolve and work of the believers. Both resolve and action are essential in the life of holiness. Good resolve needs to be carried out in work that expresses confidence in God. God is the one, however, who fulfills our resolve and gives us the energy for the work of faith. The result is that we cannot take credit for carrying them out in action.

We can rest assured that God will own us as His people in Jesus Christ—that is, because of our relationship of living for and belonging to Him.

■ *Paul prayed that God's purposes for the*
■ *church would be fulfilled in them. He*
■ *expressed his desire that glory would be*
■ *ascribed to Christ for all he would do in the*
■ *lives of believers.*

QUESTIONS TO GUIDE YOUR STUDY

1. Paul identified two dynamics of Christian living evident in the believers at Thessalonica. What were they?

2. Paul "boasted" of the Thessalonians to other congregations. What does "boasting" mean in this context? Why did he do this?

3. How will God deal with those who persecute the righteous?

4. What promise does God make to believers who suffer persecution?

This passage is one of the most difficult and problematic for the interpreter of Paul's letters. Its subject is what is known as the Day of the Lord, when the Lord will return as Judge.

The coming of the Lord will be a day of judgment. The persecutors of the church will reap the harsh punishment of being banished from the presence of God

THE PROBLEM (2:1–2)

Paul's teaching about the end-time was directed at a problem in the Thessalonian congregation. Evidently someone had told them that "the Day of the Lord" had already come. Clearly the "coming of the Lord" and the gathering of the saints to meet Him had not yet occurred. But the "Day of the Lord" could refer to a whole series of events connected with and preceding the coming of the Lord.

We may guess that the Thessalonians had been told that certain events had already transpired, which meant that the Second Coming of the Lord was about to take place. As a result, the believers were "unsettled" (NIV), or as the NRSV literally translates it, "shaken in mind." In addition, the Thessalonians also were not to become "alarmed by some prophecy" they had received.

How did this false teaching come to the Thessalonian church? Paul mentioned three possible sources:

1. By *"prophecy."* This literally means "by spirit." The word probably refers to a Spirit-inspired utterance of some sort with emphasis on the revelatory nature of

"Unsettled" and "alarmed"

"To become unsettled" used literally refers to something that has been shaken by a storm (Luke 6:48) or caused to totter in an earthquake (see Acts 16:26). The addition of the phrase "from the mind" (in the original Greek text, but not translated in the NIV), meaning something like "in mind" (NRSV), implies that Paul was worried about the believers becoming disoriented or confused by false teaching. The combination implies a spiritual instability that ought not characterize believers grounded in the truth and maturing in Christ (see Eph. 4:14).

To be "alarmed" means to be inwardly disturbed, depicting a frightened or disturbed state. The same word occurs in Mark 13:7 as a caution against premature expectation of the end. Such alarm and confusion in the face of false teaching is the opposite of standing firm in the faith.

the utterance. Prophecy, interpreted tongues (see 1 Cor. 14:5, 12), or any other exercise by which a speaker claimed to guide the church by Spirit-inspired insight could serve as the specific avenue of the teaching.

2. *By "report."* This means literally "by word." If it was intended by Paul as a contrast to "by spirit" (prophecy), it referred to speech, emphasizing its rational nature. Arguments derived by reasoning from the Old Testament or from the life of Jesus might fall into this category.

3. *By "letter."* The final possible source of the church's confusion and anxiety about the "Day of the Lord" was a letter. Possibly a letter attributed to Paul also had appeared in Thessalonica, and this may have put the apostle's authority behind the erroneous teaching.

■ *Some false teachers were claiming that the*
■ *Day of the Lord had already occurred. Paul*
■ *countered these false teachers.*

THE EVENTS OF THE END-TIME (2:3–12)

Paul immediately got to the point and told his readers that the Day of the Lord could not have come because the events associated with His return had not yet taken place. What Paul saw as the events of the end were easy to see. How they should be understood is the difficulty—one we cannot resolve with the knowledge we have.

The Main Events (vv. 3–8)

Paul identified three things that must take place before the Day of the Lord will come:

1. *A rebellion must occur* (v. 3). Paul chose not to elaborate on the nature of this "rebellion" or "apostasy." Religiously, it means to desert one's faith. This was probably an already well-defined concept for the Thessalonians. "It is not clear whether Paul means revolt of the Jews from God, of Gentiles from God, of Christians from God, or of the apostasy that includes all classes within and without the body of Christians" (A. T. Robertson, *Word Pictures in the New Testament*, vol. 4, p. 49).

2. *The man of lawlessness must be revealed* (v. 3). Paul literally described this man as "the son of destruction." This man of lawlessness would demand worship as God, display satanically inspired, counterfeit miracles, and inspire all kind of evil in his followers. "He seems to be the Antichrist of 1 John 2:18" (Robertson, p. 50).

3. *The restrainer must be removed* (vv. 6–8). "Unfortunately we do not know what Paul means by *that which retrains* (holds back), neuter here and masculine in verse 7" (Robertson, p. 51). After the restrainer's influence is removed, the lawless one "will be revealed" and his display of power will increase.

The Deceptions of the Man of Lawlessness (vv. 9–10)

His grandest delusion will be his pretension to deity. This lawless one will demand worship as God. His coming will be in accordance with the work of Satan, and the powers he will display will be impressive, but they will have their source in Satan. These works of Satan will

"Children, it is the last hour; and just as you heard that antichrist is coming, even now many antichrists have arisen; from this we know that it is the last hour" (1 John 2:18, NASB).

53

involve "all kinds of counterfeit miracles, signs and wonders."

The "Lie" (vv. 11–12)

Because of their deliberate rejection of truth, God will send those unbelievers who follow the man of lawlessness "a powerful delusion so they will believe the lie" (v. 11). The "lie" will not be just any lie but the great lie that the man of lawlessness is God (v. 12). By refusing the truth, they choose to believe "the lie."

The Truth verses the "Lie"

	THE TRUTH	THE LIE
Source:	God	Satan
Those who believe:	will be saved	will perish
Destiny of those who follow:	will share in the glory of Christ	will share in the condemnation of the son of perdition

For more information on the Lord's return, see the article, "The Return of Christ" at the back of this book.

■ *Paul's statements in this section make a*
■ *direct contribution to the question of whether*
■ *the return of Christ can happen at any*
■ *moment. Paul taught that a falling way from*
■ *God and the appearance of the man of law-*
■ *lessness will precede the Lord's return.*

CHOSEN FOR SALVATION (2:13–15)

Paul told the Thessalonians that it was God who "chose" them to be saved. The relationship they had with God was possible only because God had taken the initiative. Apart from God's choosing and calling, salvation was impossible.

Paul went on to explain the means of their salvation:

1. *"Through the sanctifying work of the Spirit"* (v. 13). Sanctification is the ongoing process of spiritual growth through the direction and power of the Spirit. It is through this process that believers become what God wants them to be.
2. *"Through belief in the truth"* (v. 13). Truth is not assent to a body of doctrine or a code of rules. The truth is personal: it is Christ. Christians believe in the truth by expressing trust in Jesus Christ.

Verse 15 is a summary exhortation. The church is to "stand firm" in the truth they had already received from Paul's teaching.

"Chose"

Chose is one of a number of words used to convey the idea of election. This is the only place in the New Testament where it is used in this sense (though it is found with this meaning in the Greek Old Testament). There is no one word which constantly expresses the idea of election, but the fundamental thought is clear. The salvation of believers rests on divine choice—not human effort. Nor was this some afterthought on God's part. He chose them "from the beginning."

Leon Morris
The First and Second Epistles to the Thessalonians, (Grand Rapids: Eerdmans, 1959), 237.

- *Paul offered thanksgiving for the Spirit's*
- *work in the life of the Thessalonian church.*
- *He also encouraged them to remain faithful*
- *to what they had been taught.*

A CONCLUDING PRAYER (2:16–17)

Paul concluded this section with a prayer for the church. Regarding the Thessalonians, Paul asked that God:

1. *Encourage their hearts.* In their present state of distress, the believers at Thessalonica were in need of divine encouragement amd comfort.

2. *Strengthen them in every good word and deed.* "Word and deed" speaks of behavior. Paul wanted the church to maintain a consistent pattern of Christian behavior. His hope was that God's strengthening of the church would allow it to stand firm against opposition and error.

■ *Paul concluded this section with a prayer*
■ *requesting encouragement and assistance*
■ *that the Thessalonians might remain firm in*
■ *the faith.*

QUESTIONS TO GUIDE YOUR STUDY

1. What problem was Paul addressing in the Thessalonian congregation in this chapter?

2. Why were the new converts at Thessalonica in a state of alarm? How did they get this way?

3. According to Paul, what three things had to take place before the Day of the Lord?

4. What did Paul mean when he declared that the Thessalonians were "chosen for salvation"?

This chapter is the last major division of the letter. After requesting prayer for his own ministry and protection, Paul expressed confidence that his readers (1) would persevere in their obedience; (2) involve themselves in proper conduct; (3) and be obedient to his teaching.

PAUL'S REQUEST FOR PRAYER (3:1–5)

Two Requests (vv. 1–2)

The apostle Paul prayed for believers. He also felt a need for their prayers on his behalf. In his prayers, he expressed no concern for things like good health, material prosperity, or good fortune. His interest was focused on his role as a minister of the gospel. Paul made two prayer requests:

1. *He asked the Thessalonians to pray that "the message of the Lord may spread rapidly and be honored"* (v. 1). The idea Paul was conveying here was *unhindered* progress rather than the effort required to make progress. Because the rapid proclamation of the gospel does not guarantee its acceptance, Paul also urged prayer that the gospel would be accepted by those who heard it.

2. *He requested deliverance from evil and wicked men* (v. 2). The word *deliver* was used to indicate future deliverance (see Rom. 11:26; Col. 1:13; 1 Thess. 1:10) and deliverance from dangers in this present age (see Rom. 15:31; 2 Cor. 1:10). The latter is what Paul had in mind here.

"Spread rapidly"

This word can also be translated *"run"* and is a metaphor taken from the world of competition in the stadium. Psalm 147:15 pictures God's Word as running very swiftly.

■ *Paul requested that the Thessalonians pray*
■ *for him and his associates. He wanted God to*
■ *bless and prosper the proclaimed word. He*
■ *also expressed his concern to be delivered*
■ *from wicked and evil men.*

Encouragement Offered (vv. 3–4)

Paul shifted from his concern regarding the persecutions missionaries would experience to the difficulties his readers would experience.

Persecution was a stark reality for the Thessalonians. Persevering in this environment required their constant realization that the Lord is faithful.

Paul then offered encouragement to those in the midst of persecution. This encouragement further described God's faithfulness: "He will strengthen and protect you from the evil one." Satan was referred to in the early church as "the evil one" (Matt. 6:13; Eph. 6:16). Likewise, Paul referred in a personal manner to the activity of Satan in his letters to the Thessalonians, both in the future (2:9) and in the present. He described Satan as a hinderer of his work (1 Thess. 2:18) and as a tempter attempting to short-circuit the faith of the church.

God's faithfulness is seen not only in judgment but also in His care for His church. Paul sent Timothy to the church with this same goal, to "strengthen and encourage" them so that "no one would be unsettled by these trials" (1 Thess. 3:2–3).

Confidence in the Lord as the one who strengthens and protects His people leads to confidence and the perseverance of the faithful. Because of God's faithfulness, believers are able to look beyond their suffering and to continue in the faith.

Thus, God's faithfulness guarantees:

- That our suffering has meaning.
- That our persecutors will reap their just reward.
- That our future is secure in Him.

■ *Paul offered encouragement to those in the*
■ *midst of persecution. It is the Lord who*
■ *strengthens and protects His people. Because*
■ *He is faithful, believers can persevere in the*
■ *faith and look beyond their period of perse-*
■ *cution, knowing that their future is secure*
■ *in Him.*

A Concluding Benediction (v. 5)

It was Paul's desire that the church live in a manner consistent with "God's love and Christ's perseverance." Christian behavior results from a genuine, inner commitment. Thus, Paul prayed that the Lord would "direct" the church in love reflective of God's love and in perseverance like that Christ had exhibited in the face of His persecutors. Paul, in effect, prayed that the church's love for God would endure and grow.

■ *Paul's benediction was an expression of con-*
■ *fidence that God would continue to direct the*
■ *paths of the believers at Thessalonica.*

"Direct"

The word *direct* is a compound word in the Greek text (the preposition "down" + the verb "to make straight"). Prefixing the verb with the preposition *down* intensifies the idea of the verb. According to A. T. Robertson, this use of the word is a "bold figure for making smooth and direct road"

A.T. Robertson, *Word Pictures in the New Testament*, vol. 4, 57.

This word "is translated 'guide' in Luke 1:79, of the Lord's 'guidance' of the feet of His people; 'direct,' in 1 Thess. 3:11, of His 'directing' the way of His servants; in 2 Thess. 3:5, of His 'directing' the hearts of His saints into the love of God."

W. E. Vine, *Vine's Complete Expository Dictionary* (Nashville: Nelson, 1996), 170.

THE PROBLEM OF IDLE CHURCH MEMBERS (3:6–15)

Paul's Exhortation and Example (vv. 6–10)

The problem Paul dealt with in this passage was that of certain members of the Thessalonian church who were living in an "idle" manner. He wanted them to "lead orderly lives" (TEV). Rather than leading orderly lives, however, they had become troublemakers.

Paul's Commands to Idle Church Members (vv. 11–12)

Paul called these idlers "busybodies." Instead of being productive individuals, they were using their time and energy to stir up trouble.

Paul commanded these idlers to "settle down" and earn their own living. This way they would not drain the church's resources and would regain respect from those in the community.

Paul's Commands to the Church (vv. 13–15)

Paul balanced his command to the idle members of the Thessalonian church with a series of commands to the church.

1. *"Never tire of doing what is right."* Literally, this command means "do not lose heart doing good." Paul urged the Thessalonians not to lose courage so they might continue to do good toward others. He wanted them to focus on doing good toward those who were idle members. Encouragement was part of his instruction for bringing idle members back into the fold.

2. *"Take special note"* of those who do not obey instruction and *"do not associate"* with idle members. For Paul's instruction to be effective, the entire congregation needed

"Busybodies"

The word for "busybody" is a compound comprised of two words: The preposition *around* and the participle *working*. It means to be "working around" or "working about" in nonproductive activities instead of tending to one's own business. "Literally, *doing nothing but doing around"*

A. T. Robertson, *Word Pictures in the New Testament*, vol. 4, 60.

The addition of the preposition *around* to the verb "implies activity that lies outside the sphere of constructive or productive labor. Such busybodies could disrupt the work of the church either with their passivity or with their activity"

D. Michael Martin, *1, 2 Thessalonians* (NAC), 282.

to participate in any disciplinary process. Offenders were to be "noted" so that a cooperative effort from the congregation could be made.

3. *"Do not regard" idle members as enemies, but "warn" them as brothers.* The church was not to treat the problem members like enemies. Rather, they were to treat these idlers as brothers for whom Christ had died, but as brothers who needed to change their ways. The church had a responsibility to "warn" any such member "as a brother" (that is, in a spirit of love and with a desire to help him).

The purpose of Paul's instruction in these verses was to bring problem members back into the fold, where they could again become productive by using their gifts and talents for the cause of Christ.

- ■ *A concern of Paul's was the inappropriate*
- ■ *conduct by some of the believers at Thessalon-*
- ■ *ica. Paul urged them to avoid a habit of idle-*
- ■ *ness, settle into productive labor, and to earn*
- ■ *their own living. He also urged the church to*
- ■ *administer firm but sensitive discipline to*
- ■ *those who rebelled against his teaching.*

CONCLUSION (3:16–18)

A Prayer for Peace (v. 16)

The conclusion to the letter contains some typical remarks. Paul was always concerned about peace in the church as an expression of the members' relationship with their Lord. Because Jesus is the Lord of peace, peace in the church would serve as evidence that the Thessalonians were under His authority. Peace is a gift that must be accepted; it is not the product of human effort.

Authenticity Assured (v. 17)

This verse contains an unusual comment. Evidently, Paul's handwriting was distinctive and easily recognized. Normally, he wrote his closing greeting in his own hand. Paul told the church that this was the "mark" (the evidence of authenticity) in every letter he had written. Perhaps the reason for this was to guard against forgery. Paul hinted even in this letter that the Thessalonians had received a forged letter (2:2).

Benediction (v. 18)

Paul concluded his letter to the Thessalonians with a benediction identical to the one in 1 Thess. 5:28, except for the addition of the word "all."

- *Paul's closing remarks expressed concern*
- *about peace in the church as an expression of*
- *the members' relationship with the Lord.*
- *Because Jesus is the Lord of peace, peace in*
- *the church would show that the Thessalonians were under His authority.*

QUESTIONS TO GUIDE YOUR STUDY

1. For what specifically did Paul request prayer? From this passage, what can we learn of his view of prayer?

2. What encouragements did Paul offer to those who were suffering persecution? How might we apply those encouragements to believers suffering persecution today?

3. According to Paul, what is a "busybody"? Why are such people disruptive to the work of God?

4. How is the church to deal with such people ("busybodies") in our churches? What should be the goal of such action?

The Lord Jesus, who was raised from the dead and ascended to the Father, will return. This conviction is expressed repeatedly in the New Testament.

The church used several terms to refer to the return of Christ. *Parousia*, meaning either *coming* or *presence*, often described the Lord's return (see Matt. 24:3; 1 Cor. 15:23; 1 Thess. 2:19). *Epipaneia* in religious usage described the appearing of an unseen god (see Titus 2:13). The revelation (*apocalypsis*) of the power and glory of the Lord was eagerly anticipated by the church (for example, see Luke 17:30; Rom. 8:18).

The phrase "the Day of the Lord" (an Old Testament theme) is also common in the New Testament. "That day," "The day of Christ," and similar phrases were used as synonyms.

Often the writer implied that he was living in the last days (Acts 2:17; 1 John 2:18). The reference to time in many passages listed above, however, is ambiguous (see 1 Cor. 1:8; 5:5; Phil. 1:6, 10; 1 Thess. 5:2; 2 Thess. 1:10). The character of that "day" is clearer than its timing. It is the day of judgment.

The Gospels. Jesus taught His disciples to expect a catastrophic conclusion to history. At that time God would effect a general resurrection and a final judgment with appropriate rewards for the just and the unjust (Matt. 7:21–27; 24:1–51; Mark 12:24–27; 13:1–37; Luke 11:31–32; 21:5–36).

Although the signs of the end receive considerable attention in the Gospels (Matt. 24; Mark 13; Luke 21), the time of the end remains obscure. Some sayings imply the end is near (Matt. 10:23; Mark 9:1; 13:30). Others imply a delay (Matt. 25:5; Mark 13:7, 10). The clearest statements indicate that the time cannot be known (Matt. 24:36, 42–44; Mark 13:32–37; Luke 12:35–40).

Acts 1:6–8 expresses the same conviction: The time cannot be known. According to Jesus, the disciples' task was to bear witness to the gospel. The time was left in the Father's hands.

The Epistles. As the church aged, questions arose. What happened to those who die before Jesus' return (1 Thess. 4:13–18)? What will His return be like, and when will it occur (1 Thess. 5:1–11; 2 Thess. 2:1–12)? What will happen to us and our world (1 Cor. 15:12–13, 23–28)? Does His delay make His promised return a lie (2 Pet. 3:3–10)?

The New Testament answers these questions with a strong affirmation concerning Christ's return. The New Testament is not clear regarding the time of His appearing. Yet the Epistles clearly reveal a persistent faith in the return of Christ (Rom. 8:19–39; 2 Tim. 4:1). His lordship is real. His victory is assured. His people will share His glory at His return (Rev. 19:6—22:17). Thus, the responsibility of the church is patience, faithfulness, and witness (see Acts 1:7–8; 1 Cor. 15:58; 1 Thess. 4:18).

(Taken from *Holman Bible Handbook*, p. 735.)

STUDY OUTLINE FOR 1 THESSALONIANS 1

   I. The Salutation (1:1)
      A. Authors and Addresses (v. 1*a*)
      B. Greeting (v. 1*b*)
  II. The Thanksgiving (1:2–7)
      A. Paul's Prayer of Gratitude (vv. 2–3)
      B. The Success of the Mission in Thessalonica (vv. 4–7)
 III. The News Spreads (1:8–10)

STUDY OUTLINE FOR 1 THESSALONIANS 2

    I. The Difficulties Confronted (2:1–2)
   II. The Purity of Paul's Motives (2:3–5)
  III. Gentle as a Nursing Mother (2:6–8)
  IV. The Unselfishness of Their Labor (2:9–12)
   V. The Acceptance of the Message (2:13–16)
  VI. Paul's Desire to Visit the Church (2:17–20)

STUDY OUTLINE FOR 1 THESSALONIANS 3

   I. The Decision to Send Timothy (3:1–5)
  II. Timothy Returns with Good News (3:6–10)
 III. Paul's Prayer (3:11–13)
      A. "Clear the Way" (v. 11)
      B. "Make Your Love Increase and Overflow" (v. 12)
      C. "Strengthen Your Hearts" (v. 13)

STUDY OUTLINE FOR 1 THESSALONIANS 4

   I. An Introductory Call to Obedience (4:1–2)
  II. Exhortations about Sanctification (4:3–8)
      A. Holiness in the Sexual Life (vv. 3–6*a*)
         1. Should avoid sexual immorality (v. 3)
         2. Should know how to control his or her own body (vv. 4–5)
         3. Should not "wrong a brother or take advantage of him" (v. 6*a*)
      B. A Solemn Warning (vv. 6*b*–8)

1. God will punish sinful behavior (v. 6b)
2. Sexual sins are inconsistent with the sanctified life (v. 7)
3. He who rejects this instruction rejects God (v. 8a)
4. Living an unsanctified life is inconsistent with the character of the Holy Spirit, who indwells the believer (v. 8b)

III. Exhortations about Brotherly Love (4:9–12)
   A. Love among Brothers (vv. 9–10)
   B. Conduct in the Community (vv. 11–12)
IV. Exhortations Regarding Those Who Have Already Died (4:13–18)
   A. "Do Not . . . Be Ignorant" (vv. 13–14)
   B. Those Who Are Alive Will "Not Precede Those Who Have Fallen Asleep" (vv. 15–18)

STUDY OUTLINE FOR 1 THESSALONIANS 5

I. The Day of Lord (5:1–11)
   A. The Thessalonians' Question (v. 1)
   B. Descriptions of the Lord's Return (vv. 2–3)
   C. Anticipating the Return (vv. 4–11)
II. Concluding Exhortations (5:12–22)
   A. Leaders and Followers (vv. 12–13)
   B. The Weak and the Strong (vv. 14–15)
   C. Optimists and Pessimists (vv. 16–18)
   D. The Cynical and the Gullible (vv. 19–22)
II. Benediction and Conclusion (5:23–28)
   A. Benediction (vv. 23–24)
   B. Concluding Remarks (vv. 25–27)
   C. Conclusion of the Letter (v. 28)

STUDY OUTLINE FOR 2 THESSALONIANS 1

I. The Salutation (1:1–2)
   A. Authors (v. 1a)
   B. Recipients (v. 1b)
   C. Greeting (v. 2)
II. Paul's Gratitude for the Believers (1:3–4)
III. The Outcome of Perseverance (1:5–10)
IV. Paul's Prayer for the Thessalonians (1:11–12)

STUDY OUTLINE FOR 2 THESSALONIANS 2

I. The Problem (2:1–2)
II. The Events of the End-Time (2:3–12)
    A. The Main Events (vv. 3–8)
        1. A rebellion must occur (v. 3)
        2. The man of lawlessness must be revealed (v. 3)
        3. The restrainer must be removed (vv. 6–8)
    B. The Deceptions of the Man of Lawlessness (vv. 9–10)
    C. The "Lie" (vv. 11–12)
III. Chosen for Salvation (2:13–15)
IV. A Concluding Prayer (2:16–17)

STUDY OUTLINE FOR 2 THESSALONIANS 3

I. Paul's Request for Prayer (3:1–5)
    A. Two Requests (v. 1–2)
    B. Encouragement Offered (vv. 3–4)
    C. A Concluding Benediction (v. 5)
II. The Problem of Idle Church Members (3:6–15)
    A. Paul's Exhortation and Example (vv. 6–10)
    B. Paul's Commands to Idle Church Members (vv. 11–12)
    C. Paul's Commands to the Church (vv. 13–15)
IV. Conclusion (3:16–18)
    A. A Prayer for Peace (v. 16)
    B. Authenticity Assured (v. 17)
    C. Benediction (v. 18)

SOME SUGGESTED BIBLE STUDY RESOURCES:

- Beitzel, Barry J. *The Moody Atlas of Bible Lands.* Moody Press
- Holman Book of Biblical Charts, Maps, and Reconstructions.
- Holman Bible Dictionary.
- Holman Bible Handbook.
- Layman's Bible Book Commentary. Broadman & Holman Publishers.
- McQuay, Earl P. *Keys to Interpreting the Bible.* Broadman & Holman Publishers.
- ———. *Learning to Study the Bible.* Broadman & Holman Publishers.

The Life and Ministry of Paul

MAJOR EVENTS	BIBLICAL RECORDS		POSSIBLE DATES
	Acts	**Galatians**	
Birth			A.D. 1
Conversion	9:1–25	1:11–17	33
First Jerusalem Visit	9:26–30	1:18–20	36
Famine	11:25–30	2:1–10?	46
First Missionary Journey	13:1 to 14:28		47–48
Apostolic council in Jerusalem	15:1–29	2:1–10?	49
Second missionary journey	15:36 to 18:21		
Letter to the Galatians			53–55
Third missionary journey	18:23 to 21:6		53–57
Letters to the Corinthians			55
Arrest and imprisonment in Jerusalem and Caesarea	21:8 to 26:32		57
Imprisonment in Rome	27:1 to 28:30		60–62
Letter to the Ephesians			60–62
Death			67

Paul's Missionary Journeys
Harmonized with the Pauline Epistles

DATE	EPISTLE	EVENT
A.D. 29	Acts	Death and Resurrection of Christ.
A.D. 32	Acts	Conversion of Paul, followed by three-year period of preaching in Damascus and Arabia. Escaped a Jewish death plot in Damascus by being lowered over wall in city.
A.D. 32	Acts	Barnabas introduced Paul to Jerusalem church.
A.D. 32	Acts	Paul returned to Tarsus.
A.D. 32	Acts	Barnabas brought Paul to Syrian Antioch. Both took famine relief to Jerusalem.
A.D. 47	Acts	I. FIRST MISSIONARY JOURNEY Syrian Antioch Cyprus—Blinding of Elymas and conversion of proconsul Sergius Paulus.
A.D. 47	Acts	Perga—Departure of John Mark. Pisidian Antioch—Paul turned to Gentiles after preaching in synagogue.
A.D. 47	Acts	Iconium—Driven from the city after preaching in synagogue.

DATE	EPISTLE	EVENT
A.D. 47	Acts	Lystra—After Paul healed a cripple, crowd tried to worship Barnabas and Paul as Zeus and Hermes. Paul was stoned.
A.D. 47	Acts	Derbe
		Lystra
		Iconium
		Pisidian Antioch
		Perga
		Attalia
		Syrian Antioch
A.D. 49	Galatians (under south Galatia theory)	Jerusalem council (Acts 15)
A.D. 50–52	Galatians (under south Galatia theory)	II. SECOND MISSIONARY JOURNEY
		Antioch in Syria
		Derbe
		Lystra—Paul took Timothy (Acts 16:1)
A.D. 50–52	Galatians (under south Galatia theory)	Iconium
		Pisidian Antioch
		Troas—Paul received Macedonian vision.
		Philippi—Conversion of Lydia and exorcism of demon–possessed girl.
A.D. 50–52	Galatians (under south Galatia theory)	Jailing of Paul and Silas. Earthquake at midnight. Conversion of jailer.
A.D. 50–52	Galatians (under south Galatia theory)	Thessalonica—Paul driven from city by mob attack on Jason's house.
A.D. 50–52	Galatians (under south Galatia theory)	Berea—Jews listened to Paul's message and searched Old Testament to verify it.

DATE	EPISTLE	EVENT
A.D. 50–52	Galatians (under south Galatia theory)	Athens—Paul preached sermon on Hill of Ares (Mar's Hill).
A.D. 50–52	1 and 2 Thessalonians	Corinth—Paul involved in tentmaking with Priscilla and Aquila.
A.D. 50–52	1 and 2 Thessalonians	Conversion of Crispus, the synagogue ruler.
A.D. 50–52	1 and 2 Thessalonians	Paul remained one-and-a-half years in Corinth after the Roman governor Gallio refused to condemn his preaching.
A.D. 50–52	1 and 2 Thessalonians	Cenchrea—Paul took a Nazarite vow by shaving his head.
A.D. 50–52	1 and 2 Thessalonians	Ephesus—Left Priscilla and Aquila behind here.
A.D. 50–52	1 and 2 Thessalonians	Caesarea Jerusalem Syrian Antioch
A.D. 53–57	1 and 2 Thessalonians	III. THIRD MISSIONARY JOURNEY Syrian Antioch Galatia and Phrygia (Derbe, Lystra, Iconium, Pisidian Antioch).
A.D. 53–57	1 Corinthians	Ephesus—Preaching in school of Tyrannus. Converts renounced the occult by burning magical books. Demetrius led riot of silversmiths on behalf of goddess Artemis (Diana). Paul ministered for three years (20:31).
A.D. 53–57	2 Corinthians	Macedonia (Philippi, Thessalonica).

Date	Epistle	Event
A.D. 53–57	Romans	Greece (Athens and Corinth)—Jews plotted to kill Paul on voyage to Palestine.
A.D. 53–57	Romans	Macedonia
		Troas—Healing of Eutychus after a fall from window during Paul's sermon.
A.D. 53–57	Romans	Miletus—Farewell to Ephesian elders.
A.D. 53–57	Romans	Tyre—Paul warned to avoid Jerusalem.
A.D. 53–57	Romans	Caesarea—Agabus warned Paul of suffering in Jerusalem.
A.D. 53–57	Romans	Jerusalem—Jews rioted against Paul in temple. He was rescued and arrested by Roman soldiers. Defended himself before Sanhedrin. Sent to Felix in Caesarea.
A.D. 53–57	Romans	Caesarea—Paul defended himself before Felix, Festus, and Agrippa. He appealed to trial in Rome.
A.D. 53–57	Romans	IV. JOURNEY TO ROME
		Crete—Paul advised sailors not to sail onto Mediterranean. Storm hit ship in which Paul was traveling.
A.D. 53–57	Romans	Malta—Paul's ship wrecked. Paul and companions remained here during winter.

DATE	EPISTLE	EVENT
A.D. 61	Philemon Colossians Ephesians Philippians	Rome—Paul is housed in a rented home. Preached to Jews and Gentiles. Waited two years for trial before Nero.
A.D. 63	1 Timothy Titus	Release from prison. Ministry in the east.
A.D. 67	2 Timothy	Reimprisonment.
A.D. 67	2 Timothy	Martyrdom.

Taken from Lea, Thomas D., *The New Testament: Its Background and Message* (Broadman & Holman Publishers: Nashville, Tenn.), pp. 304–08.

The following list is a collection of the source works used for this volume. All are from Broadman & Holman's list of published reference resources designed to accommodate the reader's need for more specific information or an expanded treatment of 1 and 2 Thessalonians. All of these works will greatly aid in the reader's study, teaching, and presentation of Paul's two Epistles to the Thessalonians. The accompanying annotations can be helpful in guiding the reader to proper resources.

Adams, J. McKee (Rev. by Joseph A. Callaway), *Biblical Backgrounds*. This work provides valuable information on the physical and geographical settings of the New Testament. Its many color maps and other features add depth and understanding.

Blair, Joe, *Introducing the New Testament*, pp. 171–76. Designed as a core text for New Testament survey courses, this volume helps the reader in understanding the content and principles of the New Testament. Its features include special maps and photos, outlines, and discussion questions.

Cate, Robert L., *A History of the New Testament and Its Times*. An excellent and thorough survey of the birth and growth of the Christian faith in the first-century world.

Holman Bible Dictionary. An exhaustive, alphabetically arranged resource of Bible-related subjects. An excellent tool of definitions and other information on the people, places, things, and events of the Bible.

Holman Bible Handbook, pp. 729–35. A comprehensive treatment that offers outlines, commentary on key themes and sections, and full-color photos, illustrations, charts, and maps. Provides an accent on the broader theological teachings of the Bible.

Lea, Thomas D., *The New Testament: Its Background and Message*, pp. 379–91. An excellent resource for background material—political, cultural, historical, and religious. Provides background information in both broad strokes on specific books, including the Books of 1 and 2 Thessalonians.

Tolbert, Malcolm O., *Philippians, Colossians, 1 & 2 Thessalonians, 1 & 2 Timothy, Titus, Philemon* (Layman's Bible Book Commentary), pp. 65–96. A popular-level treatment of several of Paul's Epistles, including 1, 2 Thessalonians. This easy-to-use volume provides a relevant and practical perspective for the reader.

McQuay, Earl P., *Keys to Interpreting the Bible*. This work provides a fine introduction to the study of a Bible that is invaluable for home Bible studies, lay members of a local church, or students.

————, *Learning to Study the Bible*. This study guide presents a helpful procedure that employs the principles basic to effective and thorough Bible study. Using Philippians as a model, the various methods of Bible study are applied. Excellent for home Bible studies, lay members of a local church, and students.

Martin, D. Michael, *1, 2 Thessalonians* (The New American Commentary), vol. 33. A scholarly treatment of the text of 1 and 2 Thessalonians that provides emphases on the text itself, background, and theological considerations.

Robertson, A. T., *A Grammar of the Greek New Testament in the Light of Historical Research*. An exhaustive, scholarly work on the underlying language of the New Testament. Provides advanced insights into the grammatical, syntactical, and lexical aspects of the New Testament.

Robertson, A. T., *Word Pictures in the New Testament*, "The Epistles of Paul," vol. 4, pp. 5–61. This six-volume series provides insights into the Greek New Testament. Provides word studies and well as grammatical and background insights into the epistles of Paul.

SHEPHERD'S NOTES

SHEPHERD'S NOTES

SHEPHERD'S NOTES

SHEPHERD'S
NOTES